Knitting Lingerie Style

MORE THAN 30 BASIC AND LINGERIE-INSPIRED DESIGNS

JOAN McGOWAN-MICHAEL

Photographs by Thayer Allyson Gowdy

Photostyling by Karen Schaupeter

STC CRAFT | A MELANIE FALICK BOOK · NEW YORK

For my husband, Mike, whose constant love, support,
and belief in me have enabled me to do what I do.
Thank you, my darling.

Published in 2007 by Stewart, Tabori & Chang
An imprint of Harry N. Abrams, Inc.

Text copyright © 2007 by Joan McGowan-Michael
Photographs copyright © 2007 by Thayer Allyson Gowdy

The following companies generously provided wardrobe and accessories for the *Knitting Lingerie Style*
photos: H&M, French Connection, and Pamela Buss Underwear

Library of Congress Cataloging-in-Publication Data:
McGowan-Michael, Joan.
  Knitting lingerie style : More than 30 basic and lingerie-inspired designs / Joan McGowan-Michael.
    p. cm.
  Includes index.
  ISBN-13: 978-1-58479-577-3
  1. Lingerie. 2. Knitting--Patterns. I. Title.
TT670.M44 2007
746.43'20432—dc22
2006025048

Editor: Melanie Falick
Designer: Anna Christian
Production Manager: Jacquie Poirier

The text of this book was composed in Fournier.

Printed and bound in China
10 9 8 7 6 5 4 3 2 1

HNA
harry n. abrams, inc.
a subsidiary of La Martinière Groupe

115 West 18th Street
New York, NY 10011
www.hnabooks.com

Contents

Introduction

Quite simply, lingerie is the very first layer of clothing a woman puts on and the last layer she takes off. It holds and shapes a woman into whatever form is dictated by the trends of the day and also symbolizes femininity, eroticism, and the mysteries of intimacy. As personal as the items themselves, the names for a woman's undergarments have taken many forms throughout history. *Unmentionables* comes to mind, as do *dainties* and *underpinnings*. It was not until the mid-nineteenth century that the collective term for them came to be known as *lingerie*, a word derived from *lin*, the French word for *linen*.

Historically, as fashion eras have come and gone, lingerie has changed form as well. If the newest styles required a wasp waist or a high, pointed bust, lingerie designers followed suit with new designs to mold the body accordingly. For example, nineteenth-century fashion dictated that a woman have a curvy torso and a tiny waist. As a result, the body-squeezing corset, a marvel of engineering, was invented. The 1920s drew away from this highly shaped look and moved toward the modern, independent flapper girl and a boyish figure. The first brassieres appeared, not to support the breasts, but to bind and flatten them into the fashionable androgynous shape. As the fashion pendulum swung and breasts again became the focus of fashion in the 1940s and 1950s, aircraft magnate Howard Hughes applied his brilliant engineering mind to the task of supporting, and at the same time accentuating, a full bust. The result was the invention of the first underwire bra.

I came of age in the 1970s, a time when feminists threw away their bras to express their freedom and the style for underthings was basic, functional, and—as far as I was concerned—boring. However, I couldn't help but notice that my mother and grandmother and the older lady who lived next door had some intriguing pieces in their drawers and hanging on their clotheslines: girdles and circular-stitched nose-cone bras, slippery satin bed jackets, seamed stockings, and strange flat pieces with hooks, grips, and rubber. Some of these items had boning and wires and such interesting construction I couldn't imagine what they were supposed to do. Some had lovely embroidery and lace, and I wondered why anyone would go to such trouble to decorate an item that would ultimately be covered up. But most of all, in my mind, these items were the essence of femininity, something I thought I'd never get a chance to share in, since the fashion for it seemed to have passed me by.

How naive I was about the cycles of fashion, how what goes around comes around again and again. By the time I'd grown up, gone to design school, and landed my first job as a designer for a major lingerie retailer, the time was ripe again for beautiful, feminine underthings. It pleased me immensely to recreate in modern fabrics the looks I'd seen in my childhood and watch them sell like crazy. Women everywhere were feeling secure enough to express their femininity again, and I was right there, at the right time, to help them do it.

In recent years, we have seen the focus of lingerie change from a supporting role to a starring one. Lingerie style is everywhere. Slips have become dresses unto themselves, cut on the bias in satin or prints and trimmed with luxurious lace. Bra straps peek out from under tank tops and evening dresses, and the bra itself is a fashion accessory, meant to be glimpsed under sheer tops and unbuttoned sweaters. Underwires and boning appear in tops and dresses with lacing that mimics the old-fashioned corsets. And thanks to pop starlets and low-cut jeans, the thong panty has made an (often literal) appearance. Truly not a season goes by that the fashion designers don't dream up new ideas for outerwear derived from lingerie.

But why hand-knit lingerie? you might ask. The answer requires no more than a peek into the lingerie drawer. Most of the garments found there are actually made from knitted fabrics albeit machine-made ones. But hand-knitted lingerie is hardly a revolutionary idea; it is simply one that is being revived. In the centuries before central heating became common, all members of a family sported hand-knit drawers, vests, long johns, petticoats, socks, and stockings to stay warm. Wool was the fiber of choice for its warmth and wicking properties.

Since warmth has become less of an issue with the advent of dependable indoor heating, we are now able to knit lingerie for the pleasure and prettiness of it without worrying about this function. We may use luxurious silks, linen blends, or easy-care cottons, with the outcome often geared most toward aesthetics. We may choose yarns for their stretch and recovery, their shine, their crispness, or simply for their indulgent softness against the skin.

While my hand-knitted lingerie may not do the heavy-duty molding and shaping of its predecessors, it can be a fun and fanciful addition to the wardrobe. In each chapter of this book, I present a basic garment—the bra, the slip, the corset, the camisole, the stocking, and more—as well as garments that contain elements of the original, but expound upon it. Some designs are truly functional, holding up breasts and stockings and lending some spice to a well-turned ankle. Some are purely for fashion and fun, daring us all to bare a little skin. All of the designs prettily remind us that to be a woman is a gift that can be celebrated every day with whatever we choose to knit and to wear.

chapter 1 THE BRA

Breasts, as any woman knows, can be rather unruly body parts. They bounce, jiggle, sway, and flop as a matter of course. Keeping their motion in check—and lending them support and beauty—is the main function of the brassiere (or bra for short). While the bra is a fairly modern device—only a hundred years old or so—the need for breast support, restraint, and adornment has existed throughout history.

In ancient Crete, for example, around 1600 BC, Minoan women contrived an early version of the corset that cinched the waist and lifted the breasts, which were left bare and painted prettily as something of a fashion accessory. In Ancient Greece athletic women bound their breasts with wool fabric for maximum support. And in early centuries throughout Europe, women downplayed their breasts by flattening them with bodices and wearing tunics.

At the beginning of the 14th century, however, with the Renaissance just under way, practicality began to give way to fashion. Women cast aside their loose-fitting robes and began to wrap their garments on the outside with long strips of leather or fabric to shape the waist and lift the bosom. During the late 18th century, a high bosom was *de rigeur*, and it was achieved with a bodice that was built inside the popular empire-waisted frocks. The 19th century is notorious for its torturously corseted feminine waistline, and those corsets did double duty in supporting the bust for almost one hundred years.

The bra as we know it first appeared in the late 19th century. And the first patent for one was issued to Mary Phelps Jacob in 1914, a clever New York debutante who fashioned, from silk handkerchiefs and ribbon, a garment to wear under a sheer evening gown in lieu of a heavy corset. She later sold her patent to Warner Brothers Corset Company (today the maker of Warner's undergarments) for a mere $1,500; over the next thirty years, Warner's made more than $15 million from the patent.

Bras have come a long way since the donning of a pair of handkerchiefs. And as you'll see in the following pages, they have become the inspiration for a whole new era of close-fitting, bust-enhancing fashions, such as the Retro Ribby Twinset, which uses accordion ridges to suggest a bra-like bodice; the Chocolate Crème Square-Neck Top, which uses an empire waist to bring attention to the bosom, and the Citrus Sun Top, which mixes the best of retro styling and bosom-y allure.

BASIC BRA

My basic bra is a pretty underwired demi-cup model, sized to fit women from 32A to 38D and styled after the designs that give French women their chic, sexy allure. For this bra to be functional, the pieces are knit in elasticized cotton yarn. This yarn allows for good stretch and recovery, properties similar to those of the fabrics used in commercial bras. You are welcome to substitute other fibers by holding a strand of your favorite yarn together with a strand of matching elastic thread (as long as the proper gauge is achieved).

As with many purchased bras, the cups are knit in two separate pieces, stabilized with an iron-on tricot lining, and sewn together. Padded tubes of fabric called channeling are sewn around the inside of each cup and underwire is inserted into it (I prefer a single continuous underwire instead of two separate wires for a barer, sexier look and simpler construction). As a final finishing touch, a satin ribbon is woven through the eyelets at the top of each cup.

No self-respecting French woman would be caught dead in mismatched undergarments, so I've added a matching string bikini.

SIZES
Bra: To fit bra sizes 32A-D (34A-D, 36A-D, 38A-D)
Panties: To fit 25 (30, 34, 38)" high hip

FINISHED MEASUREMENTS
Panties: 23 (27, 31, 35)" high hip (4"-5" below natural waist)
Bra shown measures 34B. Panties shown measure 23".

YARN
Cascade Yarns Fixation (98.3% cotton / 1.7% elastic; 100
   yards / 50 grams): 2 (3, 3, 3) balls color #7360 (MC)
Adrienne Vittadini Celia (100% silk; 109 yards /
   25 grams): 1 (1, 2, 2) balls color #537 (CC)

NEEDLES
One pair straight needles size US 7 (4.5 mm)
Change needle size if necessary to obtain correct gauge.

NOTIONS
Yarn needle
¼ yard fusible sheer tricot interfacing
Steam iron
Fabric scissors
Sewing machine, sewing needle, and thread
1 yard underwire channeling
1 continuous underwire
3 yards ¼" elastic
2 ½" plastic rings
2 ½" plastic slides
Hook-and-eye set for bras
1 yard of ¼" matching ribbon

GAUGE
20 sts and 28 rows = 4" (10 cm) in Stockinette stitch
   (St st) using MC, unstretched

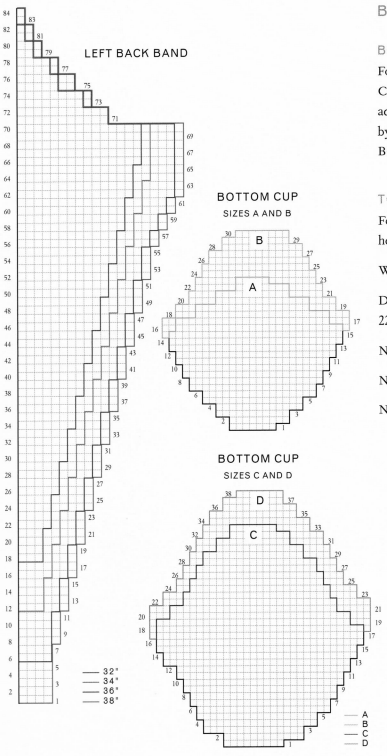

LEFT BACK BAND

BOTTOM CUP
SIZES A AND B

BOTTOM CUP
SIZES C AND D

— 32"
— 34"
— 36"
— 38"

A
B
C
D

BRA

BOTTOM CUPS (make 2)

Follow chart according to bra cup size normally worn:
CO using MC and CC held together, increase by casting on
additional sts at the end of each indicated row, and decrease
by binding off sts at the beginning of each indicated row.
BO remaining sts.

TOP CUPS (make 2)

For A (B, C, D) cup, CO 26 (28, 31, 33) sts using MC and CC
held together.

Work in St st for 3 (3, 5, 7) rows.

Decrease 1 st at each end of needle every other row 2 times—
22 (24, 27, 29) sts.

Next WS row: Knit.

Next RS row: K2 (2, 1, 1), *yo, k2tog, repeat from *.

Next WS row: BO in knit.

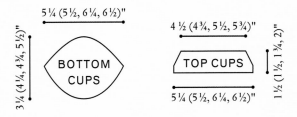

5 ¼ (5 ½, 6 ¼, 6 ½)"

BOTTOM
CUPS

3 ¼ (4 ¼, 4 ¾, 5 ½)"

4 ½ (4 ¾, 5 ½, 5 ¾)"

TOP CUPS

5 ¼ (5 ½, 6 ¼, 6 ½)"

1 ½ (1 ½, 1 ¾, 2)"

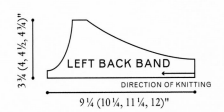

3 ¾ (4, 4 ½, 4 ¾)"

LEFT BACK BAND

DIRECTION OF KNITTING

9 ¼ (10 ¼, 11 ¼, 12)"

LEFT BACK BAND

Follow chart according to bra band size normally worn: CO using MC only, increase by casting on additional sts at the end of each indicated row, and decrease by binding off sts at the beginning of each indicated row. BO remaining st.

Using MC only, and with RS facing, pick up and knit 3 sts for every 4 rows along top of band (right selvedge, from CO row to row 70). Work in Garter st for 3 rows. BO.

Using MC only, and with RS facing, pick up and knit 3 sts for every 4 rows along bottom of band (left selvedge, from BO row to CO row). Work in Garter st for 3 rows. BO.

RIGHT BACK BAND

Work as for Left Back Band, reversing all shaping.

TABS (make 2)

Using MC only, CO 4 (4, 5, 5) sts. Work in Garter st until tab measures 2" when stretched. BO.

STRAPS (make 2)

Using MC only, CO 4 (4, 5, 5) sts. Work in Garter st until strap measures 16 (16, 18, 18)" when stretched. BO.

FINISHING

Assemble Bra: Using steam iron, fuse interfacing to backs of bottom and top cups. Trim away all excess interfacing.

Arrange bra pieces as shown in step 1. With right sides facing, machine-sew bottom edge of top cup to top edge of bottom cup.

With right sides facing, sew back band to side of cup as shown in step 2.

Add Underwire and Elastic: Apply channeling to inside of bra as shown in step 3: place sewn edge of channeling against wrong side of left bra band leaving ½" extension beyond edge of garment, machine-sew around left cup to center of

FINISHING

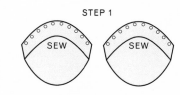

STEP 1

STEP 2

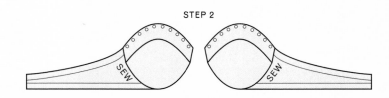

STEP 3

STEP 4

STEP 5

☐ RIGHT SIDE OF FABRIC
☐ WRONG SIDE OF FABRIC

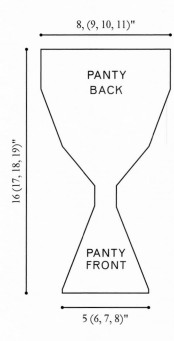

8, (9, 10, 11)"

PANTY
BACK

16 (17, 18, 19)"

PANTY
FRONT

5 (6, 7, 8)"

bra, place right cup in line with channeling, and machine-sew around right cup. Leave ends of channeling open.

Using yarn needle and CC, make casing for elastic by embroidering a row of V's (see Special Techniques—Casing for Elastic) across inside of upper and lower Garter-st borders on both back bands, as shown in step 4. Cut elastic to size and thread through casings. Using sewing needle and thread, secure ends of elastic.

Slide underwire into channeling. Fold over ends of channeling and sew securely closed. Place plastic rings on tabs and sew tabs over ends of channeling as shown in step 5.

Assemble Straps and Hooks: Place slide on strap, thread strap through ring, and secure end of strap under slide with sewing needle and thread (see Special Techniques—Strap Assembly). Sew straps to back bands, 3½" from center back.

Sew hook-and-eye set to ends of back bands.

Add Ribbon: Weave satin ribbon through eyelets at top of cups as shown. Sew ribbon ends to inside of cups.

Make a small ribbon bow and sew at center of bra.

PANTY

Using MC and CC held together, CO 25 (30, 35, 40) sts.

Work in St st for 2 rows.

Decrease 1 st at each end of needle every 4 rows 9 (10, 11, 12) times—7 (10, 13, 16) sts.

Work even for 10 rows.

Cut CC and continue with MC alone.

Increase 1 st at each end of needle every other row 10 times, then every 4 rows 6 (7, 8, 9) times—39 (44, 49, 54) sts.

Work even for 20 rows. BO.

LEG BANDS

Using MC and with RS facing, pick up and knit 3 sts for every 4 rows along left leg opening.

Work in Garter st for 3 rows. BO.

Repeat for right leg band.

WAISTBAND

Using MC and with RS facing, pick up and knit 39 (44, 49, 54) sts across back of panty, CO 25 (30, 35, 40) sts, pick up and knit 25 (30, 35, 40) sts across front of panty, CO 25 (30, 35, 40) sts—114 (134, 154, 174) sts.

Work in Garter st for 3 rows.

Next row: K2, *yo, k2tog, repeat from *.

Work in Garter st for 3 rows. BO.

FINISHING

Using yarn needle and yarn, sew ends of waistband together at right back.

Cut elastic to size and weave through eyelets. Using sewing needle and thread, secure ends of elastic.

Make a small ribbon bow and sew at center front.

RETRO RIBBY TWINSET

The 1940s was the era of the Sweater Girl. Enhancing the bustline was a major element in this curvy gal's bag of beauty tricks, and it's one I've borrowed for this design, a kickback to the era of pinup princesses. What better way to bring attention up front and center than with design elements from a bra?

The shrug features two ribbed fan-shaped fronts that barely cover the bosom. Underneath is a tank with side shaping to nip the waist and a horizontally ribbed bandeau bodice, gathered fetchingly in the center for maximum exposure. The accordion ribbing contracts or expands to give a custom fit.

FINISHED MEASUREMENTS
Shrug: 34 ½ (38, 41, 44, 47, 50)" chest
Tank: 31 (34 ½, 38, 41, 44, 47)" chest
Shrug shown measures 34 ½"; tank shown measures 31"

YARN
Classic Elite Miracle (50% alpaca / 50% Tencel; 108
  yards / 50 grams): 8 (9, 10, 11, 12, 13) skeins #3392
  Geneva blue

NEEDLES
One pair straight needles size US 5 (3.75 mm)
One pair straight needles size US 6 (4 mm)
Change needle size if necessary to obtain correct gauge.

NOTIONS
Stitch holders
Stitch markers
Yarn needle
Smooth waste yarn

GAUGE
22 sts and 30 rows = 4" (10 cm) in Fancy Rib stitch using
  smaller needles
22 sts and 30 rows = 4" (10 cm) in Stockinette stitch
  using larger needles

STITCH PATTERNS

Fancy Rib stitch

(multiple of 4 stitches plus 2; 2-row repeat)

Rows 1, 3, 5, 7, and 9 (RS): K2, *p2, k2; repeat from * to end.

Row 2 and all other WS rows: P2, *k2, p2; repeat from * to end.

Rows 11 and 13: Purl.

Repeat Rows 1 and 2 only for Fancy Rib stitch.

Ridge stitch

Rows 1 and 3 (RS): Purl.

Rows 2 and 4: Knit.

Rows 5 and 7: Knit.

Rows 6 and 8: Purl.

Repeat Rows 1-8 for Ridge stitch.

SHRUG

BACK

Using smaller needles, CO 86 (98, 106, 114, 122, 130) sts.

Work Fancy Rib until Back measures 6 (6 ½, 6 ¾, 7, 7, 7 ¼)" from beginning.

Shape Armholes: Change to larger needles and Stockinette stitch.

BO 3 (6, 6, 7, 8, 9) sts at beginning of next 2 rows, and 3 (3, 4, 4, 4, 5) sts at beginning of following 2 rows—74 (80, 86, 92, 98, 102) sts remain.

Decrease 1 st at each end of needle every other row 1 (1, 2, 2, 2, 2) times—72 (78, 82, 88, 94, 98) sts remain.

Work even until armhole measures 7 (7 ½, 7 ½, 8, 8, 8 ½)" from beginning of shaping, ending with a WS row.

Shape Shoulders: BO 5 (5, 5, 6, 6, 6) sts at beginning of next 10 (8, 8, 8, 8, 8) rows and 0 (7, 9, 7, 7, 8) sts at beginning of following two rows.

BO remaining 22 (24, 24, 26, 32, 34) sts for Back neck.

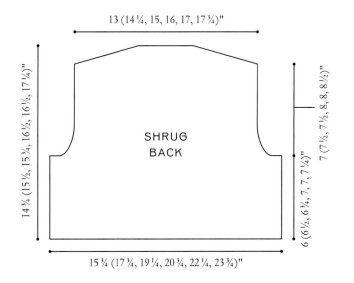

13 (14 ¼, 15, 16, 17, 17 ¾)"

14 ¾ (15 ½, 15 ¾, 16 ½, 16 ½, 17 ¼)"

7 (7 ½, 7 ½, 8, 8, 8 ½)"

6 (6 ½, 6 ¾, 7, 7, 7 ¼)"

SHRUG BACK

15 ¾ (17 ¾, 19 ¼, 20 ¾, 22 ¼, 23 ¾)"

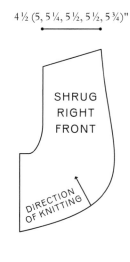

4 ½ (5, 5 ¼, 5 ½, 5 ½, 5 ¾)"

SHRUG RIGHT FRONT

DIRECTION OF KNITTING

12 (12, 13, 13, 14 ¼, 14 ¼)"

9 (9, 9 ½, 9 ½, 10, 10)"

SHRUG SLEEVE

9 (9, 10 ¼, 10 ¼, 11 ¼, 11 ¼)"

RIGHT FRONT

Using larger needles, CO 90 (96, 102, 108, 114, 120) sts.

Work Fancy Rib, decreasing 1 st at each end of needle every 4 rows 6 times—78 (84, 90, 96, 102, 108) sts remain.

Continuing in Fancy Rib, work even until piece measures 4 ½ (5, 5 ¼, 5 ½, 5 ½, 5 ¾)" along selvedge.

BO 21 sts at beginning of next RS row—57 (63, 69, 75, 81, 87) sts remain.

BO 4 sts at beginning of next 4 RS rows—41 (47, 53, 59, 65, 71) sts remain.

BO all sts next RS row.

LEFT FRONT

Work as for Right Front, reversing all shaping.

SLEEVES (make 2)

Using smaller needles, CO 50 (50, 56, 56, 62, 62) sts and work in Garter st for 2 rows.

Change to larger needles and Stockinette st, and increase 1 st at each end of needle every 6 rows 8 times—66 (66, 72, 72, 78, 78) sts.

Continuing in Stockinette st, work even until sleeve measures 9 (9, 9 ½, 9 ½, 10, 10)" from beginning, ending with a WS row.

Shape Cap: BO 3 (6, 6, 7, 8, 9) sts at beginning of next two rows and 3 (3, 4, 4, 4, 5) sts at beginning of following two rows.

Decrease 1 st at each end of needle every 4 rows 0 (2, 2, 0, 0, 0) times, every 6 rows 0 (0, 0, 2, 2, 2) times, and every other row 18 (15, 17, 16, 17, 17) times.

BO remaining 18 (14, 14, 14, 16, 12) sts.

FINISHING

Sew side and shoulder seams.

Ease Front armhole at bust by working a running stitch through ribbing at lower third of armhole, using yarn needle and waste yarn. Pull waste yarn tightly and fasten off. Set in sleeves, easing sleeve cap to fit. Remove waste yarn.

Weave in ends.

Steam garment lightly, taking care not to flatten ribs.

TANK

BACK

Using smaller needles, CO 79 (89, 99, 107, 115, 123) sts and work 4 rows in Garter st.

Change to larger needles and Stockinette st and work even for 1 (1, 1½, 1½, 2, 2)".

Decrease 1 st at each end of needle every 4 rows 5 times—69 (79, 89, 97, 105, 113) sts.

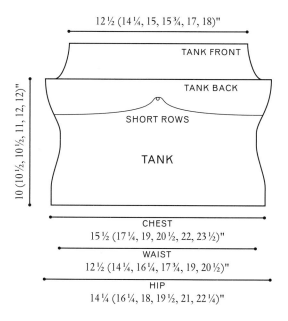

12 ½ (14 ¼, 15, 15 ¾, 17, 18)"

TANK FRONT

TANK BACK

SHORT ROWS

TANK

10 (10 ½, 10 ½, 11, 12, 12)"

CHEST
15 ½ (17 ¼, 19, 20 ½, 22, 23 ½)"

WAIST
12 ½ (14 ¼, 16 ¼, 17 ¾, 19, 20 ½)"

HIP
14 ¼ (16 ¼, 18, 19 ½, 21, 22 ¼)"

Work even for 1".

Increase 1 st at each end of needle every 4 rows 8 times—85 (95, 105, 113, 121, 129) sts.

Continuing in Stockinette st, work even until Back measures 10 (10 ½, 10 ½, 11, 12, 12)"; place Back on holder.

FRONT

Work as for Back until Front measures 7 (7 ½, 7 ½, 8, 9, 9)" and 5 sets of increases have been made, ending with a RS row—79 (89, 99, 107, 115, 123) sts.

Next Row (WS): P24 (29, 34, 38, 42, 46), pm, p31, pm, p24 (29, 34, 38, 42, 46).

Begin Short Rows:

Row 1 (RS): Knit to marker, sm, knit to 1 st before next marker, wrp-t (see Special Techniques—Short Row Shaping).

Row 2: Purl to 1 st before marker, wrp-t.

Row 3: K24, wrp-t.

Row 4: P19, wrp-t.

Row 5: K14, wrp-t.

Row 6: P9, wrp-t.

Row 7: K5, wrp-t.

Row 8: P2, wrp-t.

Row 9: K1, yo, k2tog, knit to end of row working wraps with the sts they wrap.

Row 10: Purl, increasing 6 sts evenly across row and working wraps with the sts they wrap—85 (95, 105, 113, 121, 129) sts.

Begin Ridge stitch, working 4 rows of Reverse Stockinette then 4 rows of Stockinette 4 (4, 5, 5, 6, 6) times.

Shape Armholes: Continuing in Ridge stitch, BO 3 (3, 6, 6, 7, 8) sts at beginning of next 2 rows, and 3 (3, 3, 4, 4, 4) sts at beginning of following 2 rows—73 (83, 87, 93, 99, 105) sts remain.

Decrease 1 st at each end of needle every other row 2 (2, 2, 3, 3, 3) times—69 (79, 83, 87, 93, 99) sts remain.

Continuing in Ridge stitch, work even until a total of 6 (7, 9, 9, 11, 11) repeats of Ridge stitch have been completed, then work 10 rows of Reverse Stockinette.

BO all sts.

FINISHING

Sew side seams.

Using smaller needles, CO 70 (70, 75, 75, 80, 80) sts for right strap, pick up and knit sts along Right Front armhole, knit Back sts from holder, pick up and knit sts along Left Front armhole, and CO 70 (70, 75, 75, 80, 80) sts for left strap. Work 4 rows in Garter st, then BO all sts.

Using smaller needles, CO 12 sts for center front band. Work 4 rows in Garter st, then BO all sts. Gather center front, slip band through yo hole, join ends on WS, and sew band in place.

Sew strap ends to top edge of Back.

Weave in ends.

Steam garment lightly, taking care not to flatten ridges.

CITRUS SUN TOP

I love the fashions of the 1940s. The designs, even during wartime, were clever, flattering, innovative, and even sexy. A particularly appealing category of dressing at the time was one known as "playwear." This included very casual outfits such as shorts sets, sun suits, and beach outfits. These were not swimwear per se, but they certainly showed plenty of skin, as they were primarily designed to give exposure to the sun.

My Citrus Sun Top would fit neatly into the playwear category. Since no bra would work underneath it, the shaped cups and crisscrossed straps of the top itself are designed to lightly lift the bust. Unlike those of the Basic Bra, the cups in this top are shaped with knitted-in vertical bust darts for a close fit and an eye-catching play on color, while the vertical stripes whittle a slender middle.

SIZES
To fit 26 (29 ½, 33, 36 ½)" underbust measurement, and
   cup sizes A (B, C, D)

FINISHED MEASUREMENTS
28 (31½, 35, 38 ½)" underbust
Top shown measures 28" underbust, with B cup

YARN
Louet Sales MerLin worsted (70% wool / 30% linen;
   156 yards / 100 grams): 1 (1, 1, 2) skeins #60.2555
   willow (MC), 1 skein #60.2475 terra cotta (CC1),
   and 1 skein #60.2355 mustard (CC2)

NEEDLES
One pair straight needles size US 7 (4.5 mm)
One pair straight needles size US 6 (4 mm)
Change needle size if necessary to obtain correct gauge.

NOTIONS
Safety pin
Yarn needle
Sewing needle and thread
Three ⅝" buttons

GAUGE
20 sts and 24 rows = 4" (10 cm) in Stockinette stitch
   (St st) using size US 7 (4.5 mm) needles

STITCH PATTERN

Stripe Pattern

(18-row repeat)

Using CC2, work 4 rows Garter st.

Using CC1, work 2 rows Garter st.

Using MC, work 6 rows St st.

Using CC2, work 2 rows Garter st.

Using CC1, work 2 rows Garter st.

Using MC, work 2 rows St st.

Repeat this sequence for Stripe Pattern.

MIDRIFF

Using larger needles and CC2, CO 17 (20, 24, 28) sts.

Work in Stripe Pattern until midriff measures 4 (5, 6, 7)".

Increase 1 st at the end of every other RS row 4 times—21 (24, 28, 32) sts.

Continuing in Stripe Pattern, work even until midriff measures 12 (13 ¾, 15 ½, 17 ¼)".

BO 2 sts at beginning of every WS row 6 times—9 (12, 16, 20) sts.

CO 2 sts at end of every RS row 6 times—21 (24, 28, 32) sts.

Continuing in Stripe Pattern, work even until midriff measures 22 ¾ (25 ¼, 27 ¾, 30 ¼)".

Decrease 1 st at the end of every other RS row 4 times—17 (20, 24, 28) sts.

Continuing in Stripe Pattern, work even until midriff measures 28 (31 ½, 35, 38 ½)".

BO.

RIGHT CUP

For cup sizes A (B, C, D), using larger needles and CC2, CO 31 (31, 40, 40) sts.

Work in Stripe Pattern until cup measures 2 ½ (3, 3 ½, 4)".

BO 11 (11, 16, 16) sts at beginning of next WS row to form dart—20 (20, 24, 24) sts remain.

Continuing in Stripe Pattern, work even for 2 (2 ½, 3, 3 ½)".

BO.

LEFT CUP

Work as for Right Cup, reversing shaping by binding off dart sts with RS facing.

MITERED SQUARE

Using larger needles and CC1, CO 31 sts.

Mark center st with safety pin.

Row 1 (WS): Knit.

Row 2: Knit to 2 sts before marked center st, ssk, knit center st, k2tog, knit to end of row.

Continuing to decrease 2 sts on each RS row as with Row 2, work remainder of square in Stripe Pattern, ending with last 8 rows worked in CC1.

Fasten off.

STRAPS (make 2)

Using smaller needles and CC2, CO 90 (95, 100, 105) sts.

Work 3 rows in Garter st.

Change to MC and work 2 rows in St st.

Change to CC1 and work 2 rows in Garter st.

Change to MC and work 2 rows in St st.

Change to CC2 and work 3 rows in Garter st.

BO.

FINISHING

Press all pieces lightly.

With yarn needle and yarn, sew darts in cups. Topstitch mitered square to center front of midriff, covering BO/CO edges, and sew cups to midriff, as shown in photo.

Add Buttonholes: Using smaller needles and CC2, pick up and knit 17 (20, 24, 28) sts along CO edge of midriff. Knit 1 row. Next row, work three (yo, k2tog) buttonholes evenly spaced along edge. BO.

Add Trim: Using smaller needles and CC1, pick up and knit 3 sts for every 4 rows along bottom edge of midriff. Knit 1 row. Change to CC2 and knit 1 row. BO.

Using smaller needles and CC2, pick up and knit 3 sts for every 4 rows along top edge of left end of midriff and along outside edge of left cup. Work 3 rows in Garter st, then BO. Repeat for right cup and right end of midriff.

Sew straps to tops of cups, criss-cross in back, and sew ends to midriff at intersections with cups.

Using sewing needle and thread, sew buttons to BO edge of midriff, opposite buttonholes.

Press entire garment lightly.

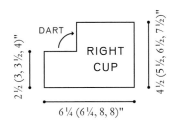

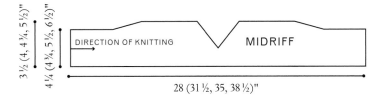

GRACEFULLY GATHERED HALTER TOP AND BOY SHORT

This playful set creates a glamour-girl look for sunning, sleeping, or lounging. Easy gathering at the bust creates a plunging neckline and a look of buxom fullness, and side shaping gives the top an hourglass fit. The boy short is brief but comfortable, designed with short-row shaping to fit a curvy derrière.

For both pieces, I've chosen a kitten-soft, hand-dyed cotton yarn that forms a modernist print all on its own. Simple Stockinette-stitch knitting throughout guarantees a satisfying sense of accomplishment in as little as one weekend.

FINISHED MEASUREMENTS

Halter: 32 (34 ¼, 36 ½, 40, 42 ¼, 44 ½)" chest
Boy short: 32 (34 ½, 36 ½, 41, 42 ½, 44 ½)" hip
Halter shown measures 34 ¼"; boy short shown
  measures 34 ½"

YARN

White Lies Designs Treasure Island Cotton
  (100% cotton; 200 yards /4 ounces): 2 (3, 3, 4, 4, 4)
  skeins Mediterranean blues

NEEDLES

One 24" circular needle size US 10 (6 mm)
One pair straight needles size US 8 (5 mm)
Change needle size if necessary to obtain correct gauge.

NOTIONS

Stitch markers
Yarn needle
Two yards 1 ½" elastic
Sewing needle and thread, for securing elastic

GAUGE

14 sts and 20 rows = 4" (10 cm) in Stockinette stitch
  (St st) using larger needles

HALTER

LOWER BODY

Using smaller needles, CO 112 (120, 128, 140, 148, 156) sts, leaving an 8" yarn tail.

Knit across 56 (60, 64, 70, 74, 78) sts, pm, knit to end.

Knit 2 more rows in Garter st.

Change to larger circular needle and join for working in the rnd, being careful not to twist sts; pm at join. These marked points are now your "side seams."

Work St st in the rnd until body measures 1 (2, 2, 2½, 3, 3)" from beginning.

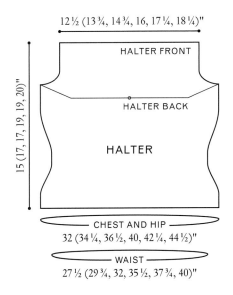

12 ½ (13 ¾, 14 ¾, 16, 17 ¼, 18 ¼)"

HALTER FRONT

HALTER BACK

15 (17, 17, 19, 19, 20)"

HALTER

CHEST AND HIP
32 (34 ¼, 36 ½, 40, 42 ¼, 44 ½)"

WAIST
27 ½ (29 ¾, 32, 35 ½, 37 ¾, 40)"

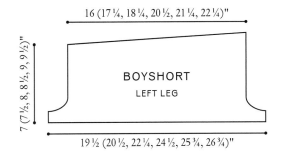

16 (17 ¼, 18 ¼, 20 ½, 21 ¼, 22 ¼)"

BOYSHORT
LEFT LEG

7 (7 ½, 8, 8 ½, 9, 9 ½)"

19 ½ (20 ½, 22 ¼, 24 ½, 25 ¾, 26 ¾)"

Shape Waist: Work 1 ssk decrease before each marker and 1 k2tog decrease after each marker every 4 rnds 4 times—96 (104, 112, 124, 132, 140) sts remain.

Work 5 rnds even.

Increase 1 st each side of each marker every 6 rnds 4 times—112 (120, 128, 140, 148, 156) sts.

Continuing in St st, work even until piece measures 10 (11, 11, 12, 12, 12)" from beginning, ending at a side seam marker.

BACK

Sm, k9, BO 38 (42, 46, 52, 56, 60) sts, k to marker, sm, k27 (29, 31, 34, 36, 38), k2tog, yo, work to end of rnd, remove marker, k9.

Working back and forth in St st, BO 3 sts at beginning of next 6 rows—56 (60, 64, 70, 74, 78) sts remain. Remove markers.

FRONT

BO 3 sts at beginning of next 2 rows, then BO 2 (2, 2, 3, 3, 3) sts at the beginning of the following 2 rows, then decrease 1 st at each end of needle once—44 (48, 52, 56, 60, 64) sts.

Work even for 2 (3, 3, 4, 4, 5)" more.

Change to smaller needles and work 3 rows in Garter st. BO.

STRAPS AND TRIM

Using smaller needles, CO 55 (55, 55, 65, 65, 65) sts, pick up and knit 3 sts for every 4 rows along right armhole beginning at upper right front, pick up and knit 3 sts for every 4 sts across back, pick up and knit 3 sts for every 4 rows along left armhole ending at upper left front, CO 55 (55, 55, 65, 65, 65) sts.

Work 3 rows in Garter st. BO.

CENTER FRONT BAND

CO 12 sts. Work 3 rows in Garter st. BO.

Use cast-on yarn tail to sew closed the slit in the bottom trim.

Try garment on and tie straps at back neck.

Pull center front band through yo hole at center front and pin in place on WS, gathering front neckline as desired. Sew band in place.

Lightly steam entire garment.

BOY SHORT

LEFT LEG

Using smaller needles, CO 68 (72, 78, 86, 90, 94) sts.

Work 3 rows in Garter st.

Change to larger needles and work in St st until piece measures 1 (1, 1½, 1½, 2, 2)" from beginning.

BO 3 sts at beginning of next 4 rows, then decrease 1 st at each end of needle every other row 0 (0, 1, 1, 2, 2) time(s)—56 (60, 64, 72, 74, 78) sts.

Work even until piece measures 4" from beginning.

With RS facing, work across 23 sts, wrp-t (see Special Techniques—Short Row Shaping), work back to beginning of row.

Next row, work across 21 sts, wrp-t, work back.

Next row, work across 19 sts, wrp-t, work back.

Next row, work across all sts, working each wrap with the st it wraps.

Continuing in St st, work even until piece measures 7 (7½, 8, 8½, 9, 9½)" from beginning at left selvedge. BO.

RIGHT LEG

Work as for Left Leg, beginning short rows on WS to reverse shaping.

FINISHING

Sew center and crotch seams to join Left Leg to Right Leg.

Using yarn needle and yarn, embroider a row of V's (see Special Techniques—Casing for Elastic) on inside of waistband to make casing for elastic, making sure that embroidery is invisible on outside. Cut elastic to desired length, and thread through casing. Using sewing needle and thread, secure ends of elastic.

Lightly steam entire garment.

CHOCOLATE CRÈME SQUARE-NECK TOP

In the sixth grade, many of the girls around me began to wear bras. Going from the thin, cotton, tanklike undershirt that every little girl wore to a bra—the province of women—was a rite of passage and a huge status symbol.

My mother, however, found it too large a leap for me and found a compromise: the camisette. This strange little garment was sleeveless, had a square neckline, and stopped right under the breasts, where it was gathered into a wide band of elastic. Alas, it had neither the cachet of a bra nor the ease of an undershirt, and I soon gathered up my own nickels, crept downtown to the five-and-dime, and purchased my own first bra.

In retrospect, the lowly camisette had some redeeming design details: an interesting neckline shape and the suggestion of an empire waist, a surefire attention-getter for a pretty bosom. I've put them to use dolling up this curvy square-necked shell, knit in a sparkly silk/wool blend yarn.

FINISHED MEASUREMENTS
33 (35, 38, 41, 44 ½, 47, 51, 53)" chest
20 ½ (21, 22 ½, 23, 24, 24 ½, 25 ½, 26)" length
Shell shown measures 33" at chest

YARN
Diakeito Diacouture Silklame (58% wool / 40% silk /
  2% polyester; 126 yards / 40 grams): 4 (5, 5, 6, 6, 7, 7,
  8) balls #915 brown (MC), 1 ball #903 lilac (CC)

NEEDLES
One pair straight needles size US 6 (4 mm)
One pair straight needles size US 5 (3.75 mm)
Change needle size if necessary to obtain correct gauge.

NOTIONS
Yarn needle

GAUGE
20 sts and 28 rows = 4" (10 cm) in Stockinette stitch
  (St st) using larger needles

If you wear a C-cup bra or larger, it is helpful to add short rows to create more room for your bust. This lengthens the center of the fabric while keeping the side seam the same length. At the designated point within the pattern, work a set of short rows as follows:

Row 1 (RS): Work to within 3 sts of end of row, wrp-t (see Special Techniques—Short Row Shaping).

Row 2: Work to within 3 sts of end of row, wrp-t.

Rows 3 and 4: Work to within 6 sts of end of row, wrp-t.

Rows 5 and 6: Work to within 9 sts of end of row, wrp-t.

Rows 7 and 8: Work to within 12 sts of end of row, wrp-t.

Rows 9 and 10: Work to within 15 sts of end of row, wrp-t.

Rows 11 and 12: Work to within 18 sts of end of row, wrp-t.

Rows 13 and 14: Work to end of row, working wraps with the sts they wrap.

Work one set of short rows for a C cup, two for a D cup, three for DD, and so on. For more even distribution, work two rows of plain St st between sets of short rows.

FRONT

Using smaller needles and CC, CO 78 (84, 91, 99, 107, 114, 123, 129) sts. Work 4 rows in Garter st.

Change to larger needles, MC, and St st. Work even until Front measures 1 (1, 1½, 1½, 2, 2, 2½, 2½)" from beginning, then decrease 1 st each end of needle every 4 rows 5 times—68 (74, 81, 89, 97, 104, 113, 119) sts.

Work 4 rows even.

Increase 1 st each end of needle every 6 rows 4 times—76 (82, 89, 97, 105, 112, 121, 127) sts.

Work even until Front measures 11 (11, 11½, 11½, 12, 12, 12½, 12½)" from beginning, ending ready to work a RS row.

Change to CC. With RS facing, knit 1 row. Work 3 rows in rev St st.

Change to MC and St st. With RS facing, using M1 increases, increase 6 sts evenly across next row—82 (88, 95, 103, 111, 118, 127, 133) sts.

Work even for 2 (2, 2, 2, 3, 3, 3, 3)". Add short rows here if desired; see Note.

Work even until Front measures 14 (14, 15½, 15½, 16½, 16½, 17, 17)" at selvedge, ending with a WS row.

Shape Armholes: BO 5 (5, 6, 6, 6, 7, 8, 8) sts at beginning of next 2 rows, then 3 (4, 4, 5, 5, 5, 5, 6) sts at beginning of following 2 rows.

Decrease 1 st at each end of needle every other row 3 times— 60 (64, 69, 75, 83, 88, 95, 99) sts.

Shape Neck: Work even for 1". With RS facing, work across 14 (14, 16, 16, 18, 18, 20, 20) sts, BO center 32 (36, 37, 43, 47, 52, 55, 59) sts, work to end—14 (14, 16, 16, 18, 18, 20, 20) sts in each front.

Attach second ball of yarn at left neck edge, and work both shoulders simultaneously until armholes measure 6½ (7, 7, 7½, 7½, 8, 8½, 9)".

BO shoulders.

BACK

Work as for Front until 4 CC rows at mid-back are completed.

Change to MC and St st. Increase 1 st at each end of needle every 6 rows 3 times—82 (88, 95, 103, 111, 118, 127, 133) sts.

Work even until Back measures same as Front at side seams.

Shape armholes as for Front.

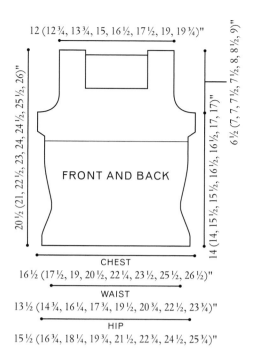

12 (12 ¾, 13 ¾, 15, 16 ½, 17 ½, 19, 19 ¾)"

20 ½ (21, 22 ½, 23, 24, 24 ½, 25 ½, 26)"

6 ½ (7, 7, 7 ½, 8, 8 ½, 9)"

14 (14, 15 ½, 15 ½, 16 ½, 16 ½, 17, 17)"

FRONT AND BACK

CHEST
16 ½ (17 ½, 19, 20 ½, 22 ¼, 23 ½, 25 ½, 26 ½)"

WAIST
13 ½ (14 ¾, 16 ¼, 17 ¾, 19 ½, 20 ¾, 22 ½, 23 ¾)"

HIP
15 ½ (16 ¾, 18 ¼, 19 ¾, 21 ½, 22 ¾, 24 ½, 25 ¾)"

Work even until armholes measure 6 (6 ½, 6 ½, 7, 7, 7 ½, 8, 8 ½)" from beginning, then shape neck as for Front.

Attach second ball of yarn at right neck edge, and work both shoulders simultaneously for ½".

BO shoulders.

FINISHING

Sew right shoulder. Using smaller needles and CC, pick up 3 sts for every 4 rows and 1 st for every 1 st around neck edge. Work 4 rows in rev St st, decreasing 1 st every other row at each corner of neckline front and back. BO.

Sew left shoulder. Using smaller needles and CC, pick up sts around armhole as at neckline. Work 4 rows in rev St st. BO. Repeat for other armhole.

Sew side seams. Steam lightly with cool iron.

chapter 2

THE SLIP

A typical slip can take many forms and serve many purposes. It may be a "full slip," worn like a sleeveless dress or used to line an equally long garment, or, sans top, it can be a "half slip," worn like a skirt or petticoat. The slip's current form bears little resemblance to its ancestors; it stems from the crinoline, a critical piece of an upper-class woman's underpinnings in the 14th and 15th centuries. This garment consisted of a cagelike construction of whalebone or tree saplings—nearly impossible to move in and necessitating the help of servants to perform housekeeping tasks (and a rich husband to pay for them all). In the 1800s, lighter materials made crinolines wearable for many Victorian women, and their width expanded to ridiculous proportions—sometimes ten feet across. With the advent of railroad and automobile travel, greater mobility was needed and so the crinoline began to shrink and was ultimately replaced by bustles and stiff petticoats, all of which were finally cast aside in the early 20th century as the androgynous flapper shape came into vogue. In their place came the pettiknicker or chemise, looking very much like the slips we know today. Made of luxurious satins and lace, these pretty underthings were designed to give a smooth, lean line under clothes.

The Great Depression brought an abrupt end to the flapper era (and luxurious lingerie), but World War II pinup girls like Rita Hayworth brought the slip back into the limelight, and the image of Elizabeth Taylor slinking around in a slip and high heels in the 1958 film *Cat on a Hot Tin Roof* caused slip sales to jump and other starlets to follow suit. Sophia Loren was quoted as saying, "There is no film star today whose underwear we have not seen." Never was this more true than in the 1990s, when the slip's transition to outerwear culminated in the slip dress, cut on the bias and clinging to every curve.

The designs in this chapter celebrate the slip's transformation from lowly undergarment to fashion statement. A stitch pattern added to the Basic Slip's traditional silhouette creates a tunic top. An antique pattern for a utilitarian garment inspires a swingy skirt in the Fit-n-Flare Trumpet Skirt. And with the One-Piece Wonder, an elasticized yarn morphs the slip into a smoothing, sexy piece of bodywear.

BASIC SLIP

When I was a child, in the day of miniskirts and go-go boots, women worried about the length of not only their skirts and dresses, but also the undergarments they wore with them. At the time, the Woolworth in my town carried slips that sported three rows of horizontal lace inserts at the hemline. The idea was that the wearer could snip off a row or two of lace and shorten the slip to match the length of her skirt quickly and without needing to sew. Being as enchanted as I was with pretty undies, I found the idea of cutting into the lace and discarding the remainder unbearable, and I could not imagine destroying a garment in such a way, especially a piece that fetched the princely sum of $2.99.

Here, I've recreated the look of those slips with drop-stitch inserts in the skirt, adding some drop-stitch detail at the neckline for good measure. This Basic Slip takes on the typical full-slip silhouette with a simple skirt, waist shaping, and a simple bra-like top. Adjustable grosgrain ribbon straps add another lingerie detail.

FINISHED MEASUREMENTS
30 (34, 38, 43, 47, 51)" chest and hip
23 ½ (27 ½, 31 ½, 36 ½, 40 ½, 44 ½)" waist
28 ¼ (29 ¾, 30 ¼, 31 ¾, 32 ¼, 33 ¾)" length to armhole
Slipdress shown measures 30" at chest

YARN
Cascade Fixation (98.3% cotton / 1.7% elastic; 100 yards / 50 grams): 6 (6, 8, 8, 10, 10) balls #7360 taupe (MC)
Berroco Zen Colors (55% cotton / 45% nylon; 110 yards / 50 grams): 1 (1, 2, 2, 2, 2) balls #8198 raku mix (CC)

NEEDLES
One pair straight needles size US 7 (4.5 mm)
Change needle size if necessary to obtain correct gauge.

NOTIONS
Stitch markers
Safety pin
Yarn needle
Sewing needle and thread
One yard ½" taupe grosgrain ribbon, two ½" plastic rings, and two ½" plastic slides, for straps

GAUGE
20 sts and 32 rows = 4" (10 cm) in Stockinette stitch (St st), using MC

STITCH PATTERN

Drop Stitch Pattern

(multiple of 2 stitches plus 1)

Row 1 (WS): Knit.

Row 2: *K1, yo twice; repeat from *, end k1.

Row 3: Knit, dropping yarn over wraps off the needle.

BACK

Using CC, CO 65 (75, 85, 97, 107, 117) sts.

Purl 1 row on RS.

Change to MC and work in St st for 6 rows, then change to CC and work Drop Stitch Pattern.

[Change to MC and work in St st for 7 rows, then change to CC and work Drop Stitch Pattern] twice.

Change to MC and work even in St st for ½".

Increase for Hip: Increase 1 st at each end of needle every 14 rows 5 times—75 (85, 95, 107, 117, 127) sts.

Work even for 3 (4, 4, 5, 5, 6)", ending with a RS row.

Decrease for Waist: Next row (WS): P20 (20, 25, 25, 30, 30), pm, p35 (45, 45, 57, 57, 67), pm, p20 (20, 25, 25, 30, 30).

Decrease 1 st at each end of needle and at outsides of markers every 8 rows 4 times—59 (69, 79, 91, 101, 111) sts.

Work even for 1", marking last row with safety pin.

Increase for Bust: Increase 1 st at each end of needle every 8 rows 4 times, ending with a WS row—67 (77, 87, 99, 109, 119) sts.

Change to CC and work one Garter ridge as follows: knit 1 row on RS, knit 1 row on WS.

Change to MC and work in St st, increasing 1 st at each end of needle every 4 rows 4 times—75 (85, 95, 107, 117, 127) sts.

Work even until side edge measures 6 (6 ½, 7, 7 ½, 8, 8 ½)" from safety pin, ending with a WS row.

Shape Armholes: BO 4 (5, 7, 7, 8, 9) sts at beginning of next 2 rows and 3 (4, 4, 6, 7, 7) sts at beginning of following 2 rows—61 (67, 73, 81, 87, 95) sts.

Shape Neck and Shoulder Points: Next row (RS): k18 (20, 22, 24, 26, 28), BO 25 (27, 29, 33, 35, 39), k to end of row—18 (20, 22, 24, 26, 28) sts in each shoulder point.

Attach a second ball of yarn and work both shoulder points simultaneously, decreasing 1 st at each edge of each shoulder point every other row 9 (10, 11, 12, 13, 14) times until no sts remain.

Fasten off.

FRONT

Work Front as for Back until Garter ridge in CC is completed.

Work remaining bust increases at outsides of markers rather than at each end of needle.

Continue to work and fasten off as for Back.

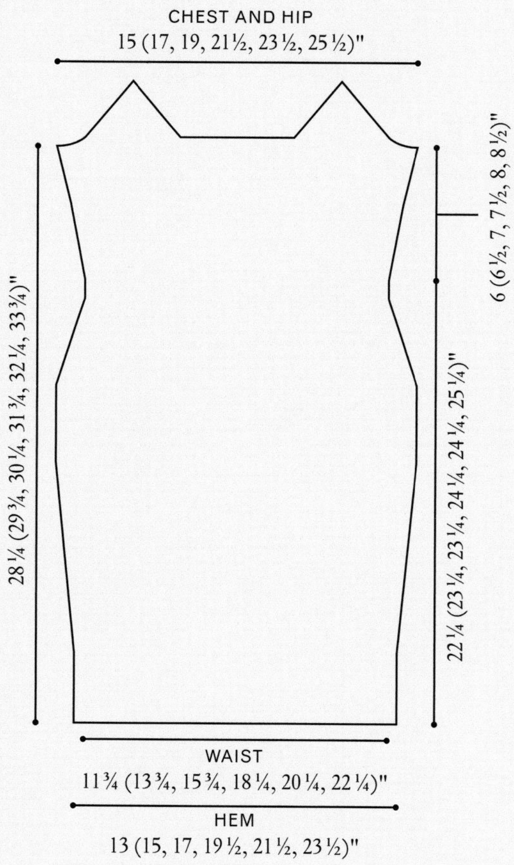

CHEST AND HIP
15 (17, 19, 21½, 23½, 25½)"
28¼ (29¾, 30¼, 31¾, 32¼, 33¾)"
6 (6½, 7, 7½, 8, 8½)"
22¼ (23¼, 23¼, 24¼, 24¼, 25¼)"
WAIST
11¾ (13¾, 15¾, 18¼, 20¼, 22¼)"
HEM
13 (15, 17, 19½, 21½, 23½)"

FINISHING

Sew side seams.

Using CC and with RS facing, pick up and knit 3 sts for every 4 rows along left front neck edge, 1 st for every BO st along center front neck edge, and 3 sts for every 4 rows along right front neck edge.

Work Drop Stitch Pattern.

BO all but last st, then pick up and knit sts across right armhole, back neck, and left armhole. Turn work, and BO all sts.

Make Front Tabs: Cut two pieces of grosgrain ribbon 2½" long. Loop through plastic rings, and sew to front shoulder points of slipdress.

Make Adjustable Straps: Cut two pieces of grosgrain ribbon 18" long. Place slide on ribbon, thread ribbon through ring, and secure end of ribbon under slide with sewing needle and thread (see Special Techniques—Strap Assembly). Sew to back shoulder points of slipdress.

Press entire garment lightly with cool iron.

PARTY DRESS WITH KNIT BODICE

During the early 1950s, corselette-and-petticoat combinations were fashionable underpinnings for the New Look created by Christian Dior. The wasp waist formed by the corselette—a strapless one-piece undergarment that carefully shaped a woman's body from the bust to the hips—and the full skirts buoyed by petticoats created the New Look's ultra-feminine and extremely popular silhouette. Inspired by that dramatic shape, I've created a somewhat casual bodice in a rib stitch to simulate the boning of a corselette and attached a bubble skirt stuffed with tulle. The combination is transformed by sparkly yarn and iridescent fabric into a one-of-a-kind party dress. But don't let this design stop with cocktail parties. The right yarn and fabric combination can alter its look significantly.

FINISHED MEASUREMENTS

31½ (34, 37, 39½, 42, 45, 47½, 50)" chest

12 (12½, 13, 13½, 14, 14½, 15, 15)" length to armhole at side seam

Dress shown measures 31½" at chest

YARN

Berroco Bling Bling (60% cotton / 38% acrylic / 2% aluminum; 92 yards / 50 grams): 5 (5, 6, 6, 7, 7, 8, 8) skeins #1536 steel/silver

NEEDLES

One 24" circular needle size US 7 (4.5 mm)

One pair straight needles size US 5 (3.75 mm)

Change needle size if necessary to obtain correct gauge.

NOTIONS

Stitch holder

Yarn needle

7 yards elastic thread

2¼ yards 54", 58", or 60" wide fabric, silvery metallic rayon

6 yards 45" wide bridal tulle in any color for skirt stuffing

Fabric scissors

Sewing machine

Sewing thread

Pins

GAUGE

18 sts and 24 rows = 4" (10 cm) in Wide Rib using larger needles

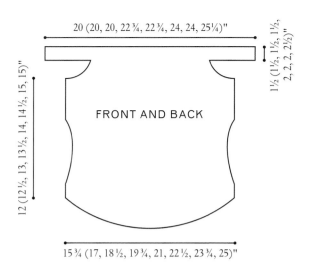

20 (20, 20, 22¾, 22¾, 24, 24, 25¼)"

1½ (1½, 1½, 2, 2, 2½)"

FRONT AND BACK

12 (12½, 13, 13½, 14, 14½, 15, 15)"

15¾ (17, 18½, 19¾, 21, 22½, 23¾, 25)"

STITCH PATTERN

Wide Rib

(multiple of 6 sts + 5; 2-row repeat)

Row 1 (WS): *K5, p1, repeat from *, end k5.

Row 2: *P5, k1, repeat from *, end p5.

Repeat Rows 1-2 for Wide Rib.

BACK

Using larger needles, CO 71 (77, 83, 89, 95, 101, 107, 113) sts.

Work in Wide Rib for 3 rows.

Continuing in Wide Rib, work short rows as follows:

Row 1 (RS): Work to within 2 sts of end of row, wrp-t (see Special Techniques—Short Row Shaping).

Row 2: Work to within 2 sts of end of row, wrp-t.

Rows 3 and 4: Work to within 2 sts of wrapped st, wrp-t.

Repeat Rows 3 and 4 until a total of 12 (12, 14, 14, 16, 16, 18, 18) sts have been wrapped.

Continuing in Wide Rib, work even over all sts for 1 (1, 1, 1½, 1½, 1½, 2, 2)".

Shape Waist: Change to smaller needles and work even for 7".

Change to larger needles and work even until Back measures 12 (12½, 13, 13½, 14, 14½, 15, 15)" along side seam.

Shape Armholes: BO 3 (5, 8, 8, 7, 7, 8, 8) sts at beginning of next two rows and 3 (2, 3, 3, 5, 6, 8, 8) sts at the beginning of following two rows, then decrease 1 st at each end of needle every other row 1 (3, 2, 1, 3, 3, 3, 4) times—57 (57, 57, 65, 65, 69, 69, 73) sts remain.

Continuing in Wide Rib, work even until armholes measure 1 (1, 2, 2, 2½, 3, 3, 3)".

Place stitches on holder.

FRONT

Work as for Back until armholes measure 1 (1, 2, 2, 2½, 3, 3, 3)"; end ready to work a RS row.

Continuing in Wide Rib, work across Front sts, CO 33 (33, 33, 37, 37, 39, 39, 41) sts for right armband, work across Back sts from holder, CO 33 (33, 33, 37, 37, 39, 39, 41) sts for left armband—180 (180, 180, 204, 204, 216, 216, 228) sts.

Join at right front and continue to work circularly in Wide Rib for 1 (1, 1, 1, 1½, 1½, 1½, 2)", ending at right front.

Next round, work a (yo, p2tog) eyelet in the center of each purl panel.

Work even for 2 rounds.

BO in pattern.

FINISHING

Assemble Bodice: Sew side seams.

To prevent waistline from stretching out, thread yarn needle with elastic thread and work 4 rows of running stitch ½" apart around inside of waist area. Secure ends.

To prevent top of bodice from stretching out, work 2 rows of running stitch ½" apart around shoulders. Secure ends.

Assemble Skirt: Lay out fabric and cut out front and front lining as shown in step 1. Repeat for back and back lining.

Sew right sides together at side seams as shown in step 2, leaving a 5" opening in side seams of skirt lining. Press side seams open.

Fold outer skirt up over lining by placing wrong sides together, as shown in step 3. Baste lining and outer skirt together around upper edge.

Pleat skirt as shown in step 4, pinning each pleat in place. Try skirt on dress form or the intended recipient, pinning top of skirt to fit waist area closely.

Assemble Dress: Put bodice on over skirt, and smooth down over pleats. Arrange pleats in a pleasing fashion, and pin bodice to skirt. Machine-sew bodice to skirt using two lines of straight stitching. Trim away excess fabric at inside waist of skirt.

Cut necktie as shown in step 5. Fold in half lengthwise with right sides together, and stitch ¼" in from edge leaving one end open for turning. Turn necktie right side out, press, and slip-stitch end closed. Weave through eyelets at upper edge of front bodice as shown, then through two eyelets at center back and tie.

Cut bridal tulle into ½-yard pieces, crumple, and stuff through bottom openings in lining to fill out bottom of bubble skirt. Slip-stitch openings closed. Remove bridal tulle for laundering.

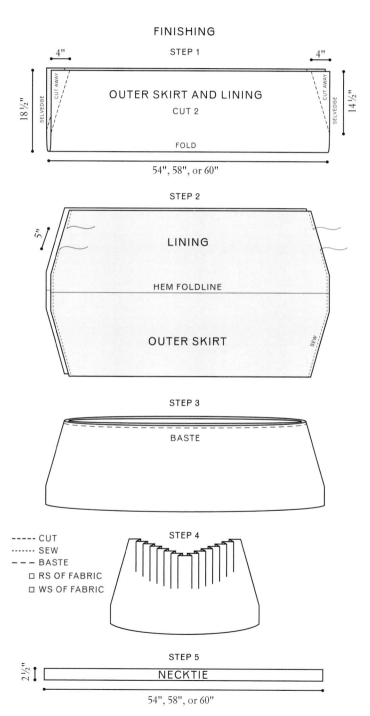

FINISHING

STEP 1

4"   4"

OUTER SKIRT AND LINING
CUT 2

18½"   SELVEDGE   CUT AWAY   CUT AWAY   SELVEDGE   14½"

FOLD

54", 58", or 60"

STEP 2

5"

LINING

HEM FOLDLINE

OUTER SKIRT   SEW

STEP 3

BASTE

----- CUT
······ SEW
– – – BASTE
☐ RS OF FABRIC
☐ WS OF FABRIC

STEP 4

STEP 5

2½"   NECKTIE

54", 58", or 60"

SILK SLIP

The slip has evolved to become just about everything except an undergarment. We sleep and lounge in it, wear it with sandals as a sundress, and throw on a shawl or fancy shrug and call it evening wear. The slip definitely earned a place in fashion history in 1996, on the day that Carolyn Bessette married John F. Kennedy, Jr., wearing a fabulous heavy satin rendition of the slip dress. It was, after decades of lace and pearl embellishment on wedding wear, almost shocking in its simplicity and beauty.

This slip is a lingerie version of itself, knit in a pale pink hand-dyed silk/wool yarn combined with a silky bias-cut fabric skirt. Feel free to experiment with different yarn and fabric combinations as well as skirt lengths. Keep it short for flirty lounge- or party-wear, or add a long, clinging skirt anytime you'd like to make a glamorous impression.

SIZES
To fit 26 (29 ½, 33, 36 ½, 38 ½)" underbust measurement,
and cup sizes A (B, C, D)

FINISHED MEASUREMENTS
27 ¾ (31 ½, 35, 38 ½, 40 ½)" underbust
19 (20, 21, 22, 23)" long at side seam
Slip shown fits 26" underbust, with C cup

YARN
White Lies Designs Interlude (50% silk / 50% merino
wool; 90 yards / 42 grams): 2 (3, 3, 4, 4) skeins
antique pink

NEEDLES
One pair straight needles size US 7 (4.5 mm)
Change needle size if necessary to obtain correct gauge.

NOTIONS
Yarn needle
Crochet hook size US H/8 (5 mm)
½ yard sheer fusible tricot interfacing
Steam iron
Fabric scissors
Sewing needle and thread
Sewing machine
One large sheet tissue paper
2 ½ yards 45" wide silk charmeuse or other silky blouse-
weight woven fabric
2 yards matching ½" lace trim
One set hook-and-eye skirt closure
Two ½" plastic rings and two ½" plastic slides

GAUGE
20 sts and 28 rows = 4" (10 cm) in Stockinette stitch (St st)

STITCH PATTERN

Vine Lace

(from *A Treasury of Knitting Patterns* by Barbara G. Walker)
(multiple of 9 sts + 4; 4-row repeat) (See Chart)

Row 1 (RS): K2, *k1, yo, k2, ssk, k2tog, k2, yo; repeat from *, end k2.

Rows 2 and 4: Purl.

Row 3: K2, *yo, k2, ssk, k2tog, k2, yo, k1, repeat from *, end k2.

MIDRIFF

CO 139 (157, 175, 193, 202) sts.

Work 4 repeats of Vine Lace.

Change to St st and BO 63 (72, 81, 90, 95) sts at beginning of next 2 rows—13 (13, 13, 13, 12) sts remain.

Decrease 1 st at each end of needle every other row 3 times—7 (7, 7, 7, 6) sts remain.

BO.

RIGHT CUP

For cup sizes A (B, C, D), CO 31 (31, 40, 40) sts.

Work 4 repeats of Vine Lace.

Change to St st and work even until cup measures 2 ½ (3, 3 ½, 4)" from beginning.

BO 11 (11, 16, 16) sts at beginning of next WS row to form dart.

Continuing in St st, work even for 2 (2 ½, 3, 3 ½)".

BO.

9-ST REPEAT

□ KNIT ON RS, PURL ON WS
○ YO
⊠ K2TOG
⊠ SSK

MIDRIFF

1 ¼"

28 (31 ½, 35, 38 ½, 40 ½)"

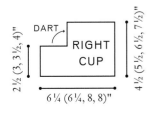

DART

RIGHT CUP

2 ½ (3, 3 ½, 4)"

4 ½ (5 ½, 6 ½, 7 ½)"

6 ¼ (6 ¼, 8, 8)"

LEFT CUP

Work as for Right Cup, reversing shaping by binding off dart sts with RS facing.

FINISHING

Steam block midriff and cups lightly, taking care to open up lace and spread out scallop edges.

Crochet Edges and Straps: Sc along side edge of Right Cup from bottom to top, then chain for 20". Turn and work back in sc. Fasten off.

Chain 20", then sc along side edge of Left Cup from top to bottom. Turn and work back in sc. Fasten off.

Assemble Bodice: With steam iron, fuse interfacing to backs of all three pieces. Trim interfacing to edges of knitting.

Sew cup darts by hand with sewing needle and thread, or by machine.

With right sides together, sew cups to midriff by hand or by machine.

Assemble Skirt: Trace skirt shape onto tissue paper according to measurements selected, and cut out pattern piece. Fold fabric in half as shown and place pattern piece on the bias. Cut out skirt pieces. Machine-sew side seams, leaving ½" seam allowances and stretching seam very slightly when sewing. Press seams to one side.

Cut a 7" x 1¼" rectangle of fabric on the bias for use as bias tape. Mark center back of skirt and cut a 3" slit at the upper back edge. With right sides together, sew bias tape around edges of slit. Wrap bias tape around edges of slit, and sew to inside.

Sew lace trim around bottom edge of skirt.

Press skirt.

Assemble Slip: Sew skirt to midriff, stitching through scallops and leaving a 1" extension at each end of midriff.

Sew hook-and-eye closure to extensions, overlapping extensions so that edges of the slit just touch each other neatly.

Make Adjustable Straps: Sew rings to back of slip on either side of center third of back of slip. Place slide on right strap, thread strap through ring, and secure end of strap under slide with sewing needle and thread (see Special Techniques—Strap Assembly). Repeat for left strap.

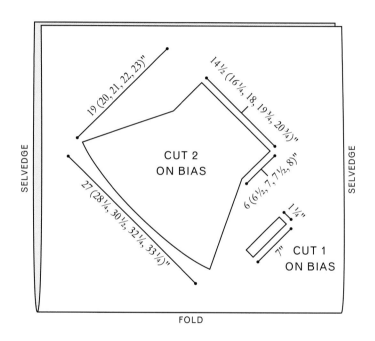

☐ RIGHT SIDE OF FABRIC
☐ WRONG SIDE OF FABRIC

FIT-N-FLARE TRUMPET SKIRT

There is no sexier skirt silhouette than the trumpet shape. It hugs the hips and thighs, flows around the knees, and exposes a pretty ankle. The motion it makes while walking is a sensuous swish.

This version was inspired by the knitted petticoats women wore for warmth in the late 19th and early 20th centuries. Adapted from antique knitting patterns of that time, it's fitted at the top (originally to give less bulk under a corset) and flared at the bottom to fill out the bell shaping. Circularly knit, my rendition has the added bonus of openwork ladder-stitch lines, giving the skirt a gored look to punctuate curves and emphasize the vertical line. Pretty little glass leaves trim the ends of the drawstring tie.

FINISHED MEASUREMENTS
28 ½ (32, 35 ½, 39, 42 ¾)" waist, prior to elastic insertion
33 ¾ (38, 42 ¼, 46 ½, 50 ¾)" hip
26 (26, 27, 27, 28)" length
Skirt shown measures 28 ½" at waist

YARN
Diakeito Diarufuran (100% wool; 161 yards / 40 grams):
  7 (8, 9, 10, 11) balls color #212

NEEDLES
One 24" circular needle size US 9 (5.5 mm)
Change needle size if necessary to obtain correct gauge.

NOTIONS
Stitch markers
Yarn needle
Six ½" decorative glass beads, pink and brown multi
1 ½ yards 1" skirt elastic
Sewing needle and thread

GAUGE
18 sts and 24 rows = 4" (10 cm) in Stockinette stitch
  (St st)

SKIRT

CO 128 (144, 160, 176, 192) sts. Join for working in the rnd, being careful not to twist sts; place marker (pm) for beginning of rnd.

Work in Garter st for 6 rnds, placing a st marker after every 16 sts on the last rnd.

Next rnd: work across 64 (72, 80, 88, 96) sts, work (yo, k2tog) for drawstring eyelet, work to end of rnd.

Continuing in Garter st, work even until waistband measures 1" from beginning, ending ready to work a knit rnd. Work an increase rnd as follows: *sm, M1, knit to next marker; repeat from * to end—136 (153, 170, 187, 204) sts.

Continuing in Garter st, work even until skirt measures 2" from beginning, ending ready to work a knit rnd. Work an increase rnd—144 (162, 180, 198, 216) sts.

Continuing in Garter st, work even until skirt measures 2 ½ (2 ½, 3, 3, 3 ½)" from beginning, then work as follows:

Rnd 1: *Sm, yo, k2tog, knit to next marker; repeat from *.

Rnd 2: Knit.

Repeat Rnds 1 and 2.

Continuing in established pattern, work even until skirt measures 4 (4 ½, 5, 5, 5 ½)" from beginning, ending ready to work a plain knit rnd. Work an increase rnd—152 (171, 190, 209, 228) sts.

Continuing in established pattern, work even until skirt measures 17 (17, 18, 18, 19)" from beginning, then work as follows:

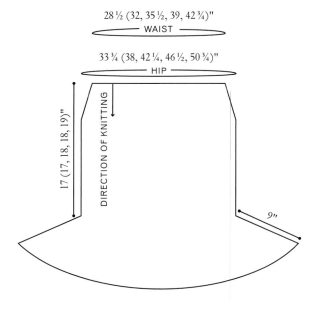

28 ½ (32, 35 ½, 39, 42 ¾)"
WAIST

33 ¾ (38, 42 ¼, 46 ½, 50 ¾)"
HIP

17 (17, 18, 18, 19)"

DIRECTION OF KNITTING

9"

Rnd 3: *Sm, yo, knit to next marker, repeat from *—160 (180, 200, 220, 240) sts.

Rnd 4: Knit.

Repeat Rnds 3 and 4—168 (188, 208, 228, 248).

Continue in established pattern until each section contains 45 sts—360 (405, 450, 495, 540) sts; end having worked Rnd 4. Note: To lengthen skirt, work more rnds here, continuing to increase in each section.

Change to Garter st and increase as follows:

Rnd 5: *Sm, M1, knit to next marker; repeat from * .

Rnd 6: Purl.

Repeat Rnds 5 and 6 until each section contains 50 sts—400 (450, 500, 550, 600) sts on needles. BO.

FINISHING

Using yarn needle and yarn, embroider a row of V's 1¼" tall (see Special Techniques—Casing for Elastic) on inside of waistband to make casing for drawstring and elastic, making sure that embroidery is invisible on outside.

Make drawstring as follows: CO 4 sts. Work back and forth in St st until drawstring measures 46" or desired length. BO.

Thread drawstring through casing and pull ends out of eyelet hole. Cut elastic to desired length, and thread through casing. Using sewing needle and thread, secure ends of elastic and sew beads onto ends of drawstring.

ONE-PIECE WONDER

I call this design the One-Piece Wonder because it serves the purpose of four undergarments: It smoothes the torso like a slip, uplifts and enhances the bust like an underwire bra, holds up stockings like a garter belt, and gives the coverage of a panty. I've based it on its 1920s forebear the cami-knicker, a lingerie piece that combined a camisole with short pants that fastened at the crotch.

Traditionally, commercial body-shaping garments, such as girdles and longline bras, have been fairly basic in design, but I've dressed this one up with a silk yarn combined with elasticized cotton and a tulle ruffle at the bust. The combination gives just the right amount of vintage appeal along with sleek modern functionality. Partnered with a dressy skirt and cardigan, you'll have a perfect lingerie-inspired evening look, or wear it completely undercover for a functional piece of underpinning.

SIZES
To fit bra sizes 32A-D (34A-D, 36A-D, 38A-D) and full
  hip sizes 33-34¾ (35-36¾, 37-38¾, 39-40¾)"

FINISHED MEASUREMENTS
23 (27, 31, 35)" high hip (4"-5" below natural waist)
Bodysuit shown measures 32C, 23" high hip.

YARN
Cascade Yarns Fixation (98.3% cotton / 1.7% elastic; 100
  yards / 50 grams): 5 (6, 6, 7) balls color #2137 (MC)
Adrienne Vittadini Celia (100% silk; 109 yards / 25
  grams): 5 (6, 6, 7) balls color #4543 (CC)

NEEDLES
One pair straight needles size US 7 (4.5 mm)
Change needle size if necessary to obtain correct gauge.

NOTIONS
Yarn needle
¼ yard fusible sheer tricot interfacing
Steam iron
Fabric scissors
Sewing machine, sewing needle, and thread
1 yard underwire channeling
1 continuous underwire
3 yards ¼" elastic
2 ½" plastic rings
2 ½" plastic slides
Set of 4 garter grips and 4 garter slides
Hook-and-eye tape, 3 hooks and 3 eyes 1" apart
¼ yard matching bridal tulle
3 matching ribbon rosettes

GAUGE
20 sts and 28 rows = 4" (10 cm) in Stockinette stitch
  (St st) using MC, unstretched

High hip is measured around hip bones at approximately 5-6" below natural waist. Full hip is measured around fullest part of hips at 8-9" below natural waist.

BOTTOM CUPS (make 2)

Follow chart according to bra cup size normally worn: CO using MC and CC held together, increase by casting on additional sts at the end of each indicated row, and decrease by binding off sts at the beginning of each indicated row. BO remaining sts.

TOP CUPS (make 2)

For A (B, C, D) cup, CO 26 (28, 31, 33) sts using MC and CC held together.

Work in St st for 3 (3, 5, 7) rows.

Decrease 1 st at each end of needle every other row 2 times—22 (24, 27, 29) sts.

Work in St st for 4 more rows. BO.

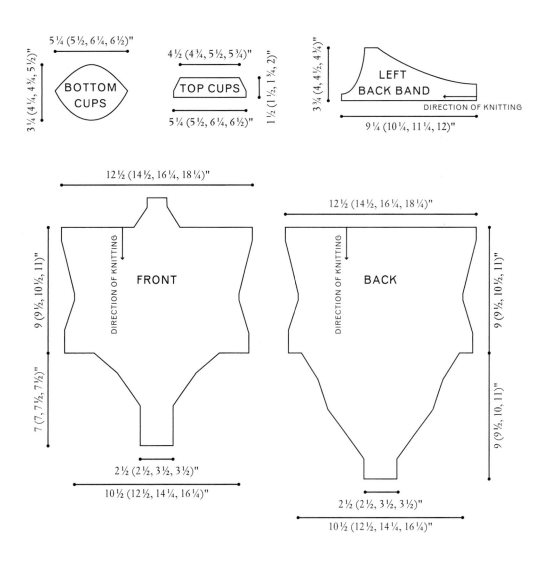

LEFT BACK BAND

Follow chart according to bra band size normally worn:
CO using MC and CC held together, increase by casting on
additional sts at the end of each indicated row, and decrease
by binding off sts at the beginning of each indicated row.
BO remaining st.

Using MC only, and with RS facing, pick up and knit 3 sts for
every 4 rows along top of band (right selvedge, from CO row
to row 70). Work in Garter st for 3 rows. BO.

Using MC only, and with RS facing, pick up and knit 3 sts for
every 4 rows along bottom of band (left selvedge, from BO
row to CO row). Work in Garter st for 3 rows. BO.

RIGHT BACK BAND

Work as for Left Back Band, reversing all shaping.

TABS (make 2)

Using MC only, CO 4 (4, 5, 5) sts. Work in Garter st until tab
measures 2" when stretched. BO.

STRAPS (make 2)

Using MC only, CO 4 (4, 5, 5) sts. Work in Garter st until
strap measures 16 (16, 18, 18)" when stretched. BO.

FRONT

Beginning at upper center front and working downward, CO
7 sts using MC and CC held together.

For A (B, C, D) cup, work in St st for 4 (6, 6, 8) rows.

Increase 1 st at each end of needle every other row 5 times—
17 sts.

CO 23 (28, 32, 37) sts at the end of the next 2 rows—63 (73,
81, 91) sts.

Work even in St st for 1".

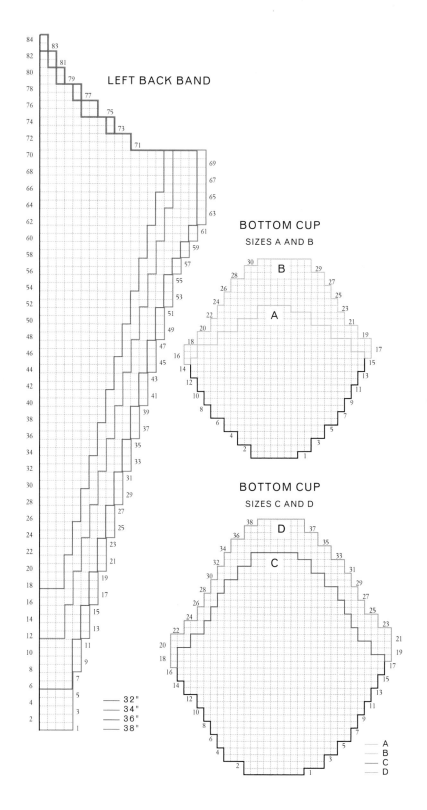

Shape Waist: Decrease 1 st at each end of needle every 6 rows 5 times—53 (63, 71, 81) sts.

Work even until Front measures 5 (5 ½, 6, 6 ½)" from base of bra (not from start of center front tab).

Increase 1 st at each end of needle every 4 rows 4 times—61 (71, 79, 89) sts.

Work even until Front measures 9 (9 ½, 10 ½, 11)" from base of bra (not from start of center front tab).

Shape Leg Openings: BO 9 (12, 11, 14) sts at beginning of next 2 rows, BO 2 sts at beginning of following 10 (8, 12, 16) rows, then decrease 1 st at each end of needle every other row 5 (9, 8, 6) times—13 (13, 17, 17) sts.

Work even until Front measures 7 (7, 7 ½, 7 ½)" from first leg-opening BO. BO.

BACK

Using MC and CC held together, CO 63 (73, 81, 91) sts.

Work even in St st for 1".

Shape Waist: Decrease 1 st at each end of needle every 6 rows 5 times—53 (63, 71, 81) sts.

Work even until Back measures 5 (5 ½, 6, 6 ½)".

Increase 1 st at each end of needle every 4 rows 4 times—61 (71, 79, 89) sts.

Work even until Back measures 9 (9 ½, 10 ½, 11)".

Shape Leg Openings: BO 2 (6, 8, 10) sts at beginning of next two rows—57 (59, 63, 79) sts.

Decrease 1 st at each end of needle every other row 6 (6, 6, 12) times, then every 4 rows 4 (4, 4, 3) times, then every other row 12 (13, 13, 16) times—13 (13, 17, 17) sts.

Work even until Back measures 9 (9 ½, 10, 11)" from first leg-opening BO. BO.

SUSPENDERS (make 4)

Using MC only, CO 4 sts. Work in Garter st until suspender measures 9" when stretched. BO.

FINISHING

Sew Front to Back at side seams.

Using MC and with RS facing, pick up and knit 3 sts for every 4 rows along left leg opening. Working in Garter st, knit 3 rows. BO. Repeat for right leg band.

Assemble Bra: Using yarn needle and CC, sew back bands together at center back, then make casing for elastic by embroidering a row of V's (see Special Techniques—Casing for Elastic) across inside of upper and lower Garter-st borders, as shown in step 1.

Sew back bands to top of body as shown in step 2.

Using steam iron, fuse interfacing to backs of bottom and top cups. Trim away all excess interfacing. With right sides facing, machine-sew bottom edge of top cup to top edge of bottom cup, then sew cup to body as shown in step 3.

Apply channeling to inside of bra as shown in step 4: place sewn edge of channeling against wrong side of left bra band leaving a ½" extension beyond edge of garment, machine-sew around left cup to tab at center front of body, then machine-sew channeling across tab and around right cup. Leave ends of channeling open.

Cut elastic to size and thread through casings. Using sewing needle and thread, secure ends of elastic.

Slide underwire into channeling. Fold over ends of channeling and sew securely closed. Place plastic rings on tabs and sew tabs over ends of channeling as shown in step 5.

Place slide on strap, thread strap through ring, and secure end of strap under slide with sewing needle and thread (see Special Techniques—Strap Assembly). Sew straps to back bands, 3 ½" from center back.

Add Suspenders and Hooks: Place slide on suspender strap, thread strap through garter grip, and secure end of strap under slide with sewing needle and thread (see Special Techniques—Suspender Assembly). Sew suspenders onto legs, 2" from side seam in back and 3" from side seam in front.

Cut hook-and-eye tape to size and sew onto Front and Back at crotch.

Add Tulle and Rosettes: Cut tulle into 2 strips 2 ½" wide and 45" long. Fold each strip in half and pleat, basting with needle and thread. Sew ruffling to upper edge of bra cup.

Sew ribbon rosettes at center front and at straps, as shown.

FINISHING

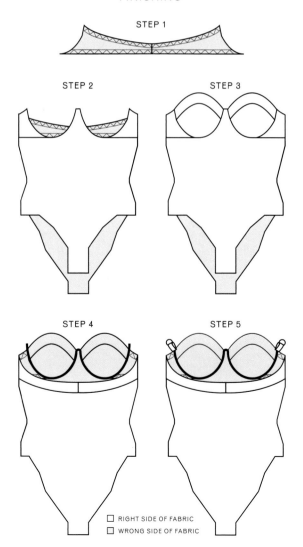

STEP 1

STEP 2   STEP 3

STEP 4   STEP 5

☐ RIGHT SIDE OF FABRIC
☐ WRONG SIDE OF FABRIC

chapter 3 THE CORSET

Few garments give the phrase "beauty must suffer" as much meaning as the corset. For the past 350 years, a tiny waist and full round hips have come to symbolize sexual maturity and fertility and, as an extension of those, desirability. The drive for a woman to maintain this youthful shape has kept the corset in the spotlight, though in ever kinder, gentler, and sexier forms—bustiers, girdles, corselettes, and merry widows all stem from the corset.

Corsetry reached its zenith in the 16th century with Catherine de Medici, wife of Henry II, who proclaimed the ideal waist circumference to be thirteen inches. This was achieved with a garment called the iron maiden, literally fashioned from metal panels that gave it the appearance of battle armor. Worn over a tightly laced fabric undergarment, it compacted the midsection, severely curtailing the wearer's ability to move and causing fainting, cracked ribs, pierced livers, even death. Corsets were abandoned briefly after the French Revolution but returned with a vengeance in the 1800s, during which they became complicated steel-boned, leather-encased affairs.

The torture continued until the early 1900s, when in America, suffragettes rejected the corset for its symbolic repression, and younger generations found it impossible to tango while corseted. WWI eliminated the corset for good as women joined the workforce in unprecedented numbers, taking jobs that required flexibility and stamina. The War Industries Board issued a call for women to stop buying metal-boned corsets, saving 28,000 tons of metal in 1917—enough to build two battleships.

Modified versions of the corset have gone in and out of fashion throughout the 20th century. The corselette, a relatively comfortable combination of corset and bra, became the foundation of Christian Dior's New Look of the late 1940s and 1950s. Dior's corselettes became so fancy that they were worn as evening wear, a trend that was revived in the 1980s by designers such as Jean-Paul Gaultier and Vivienne Westwood and rockers like Madonna and Cyndi Lauper.

All of the corsets in this chapter are also meant to be seen, but each gives a wink to a time when its appearance on the street would have created a scandal. While a knitted version of the corset may not take control of the body in the way its ancestors did, the look is still pretty, feminine, and, yes, sexy.

BASIC CORSET

As you might expect, a knitted corset doesn't have the kind of constricting power it would take to whittle a thirteen-inch waist—thank goodness. However, knitted corsets offer other benefits—including gentle shaping and feminine details—that make them wonderful to wear.

My version of the Basic Corset is worked in a cotton/elastic blend yarn with vertical lines and short-row insets knit in a pretty ribbon yarn, providing contrast and curvy shaping. Many of the 19th-century corset styles were based on this structure: a tubular shape with pie-shaped wedges of fabric inset where the body was the fullest—the hips and breasts. Inside, channeling is hand-sewn to sections of the front, into which plastic boning is inserted for structure—a much more forgiving option than the steel boning of old, which forced a woman to stand and sit with arrow-straight posture.

Wear this over bare skin, as we've shown here, or hook it over a white shirt or tee instead of a vest for a lingerie-as-outerwear twist and a great way to show off some curves.

SIZES
To fit 31-33 (35-37, 39-41, 43-45)" chest

FINISHED MEASUREMENTS
30 (34, 38, 42)" chest
24 (28, 32, 37)" waist
30 (34, 38, 42)" hip
Corset shown measures 30" at chest

YARN
Cascade Fixation (98.3% cotton / 1.7% elastic; 100 yards / 50 grams): 4 (4, 5, 5) balls #7360 taupe (MC)
Berroco Zen Colors (55% cotton / 45% nylon; 110 yards / 50 grams): 1 ball #8108 raku mix (CC)

NEEDLES
One pair straight needles size US 7 (4.5 mm)
One pair straight needles size US 6 (4 mm)
Change needle size if necessary to obtain correct gauge.

NOTIONS
Safety pins
Yarn needle
½ yard ¼" elastic
Sewing machine, sewing needle, and thread
½ yard hook-and-eye tape
3 yards channeling for boning
6 pieces 16" plastic boning

GAUGE
20 sts and 28 rows = 4" (10 cm) in Stockinette stitch (St st)

STITCH PATTERNS

Bust Dart

Rows 1 and 25 (RS): K3, wrp-t (see Special Techniques— Short Row Shaping).

Row 2 and all other even-numbered rows through Row 26: Purl.

Rows 3 and 23: K6, wrp-t.

Rows 5 and 21: K9, wrp-t.

Rows 7 and 19: K12, wrp-t.

Rows 9 and 17: K15, wrp-t.

Rows 11 and 15: K18, wrp-t.

Row 13: K21, wrp-t.

Hip Dart

Row 1 and all other odd-numbered rows through Row 11 (RS): Knit.

Rows 2 and 10: P6, wrp-t.

Rows 4 and 8: P12, wrp-t.

Row 6: P18, wrp-t.

Row 12: Knit.

RIGHT SIDE

Using MC and larger needles, CO 60 (60, 65, 65) sts.

Work 6 rows in Garter st.

Work 2 (6, 10, 14) rows in St st.

Change to CC and work 2 rows in Garter st.

Change to MC and work 6 rows in St st.

Change to CC and work 2 rows in Garter st.

Work first bust dart.

Work first hip dart.

Work 2 rows in Garter st.

[Change to MC and work 6 rows in St st, then change to CC and work 2 rows in Garter st] twice.

Work second hip dart.

Work 2 rows in Garter st.

BACK

Change to MC and St st.

Decrease 1 st at beginning of every RS row 5 times, then every other RS row 5 times — 50 (50, 55, 55) sts.

Place safety pins at both edges of work.

Continuing in St st, work even 5 (6, 7, 8)".

Place safety pins at both edges of work.

Increase 1 st at beginning of every other RS row 5 times, then every RS row 5 times—60 (60, 65, 65) sts.

LEFT SIDE

Change to CC and work 2 rows in Garter st.

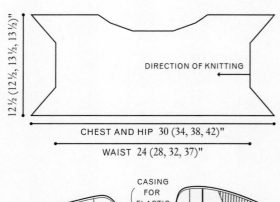

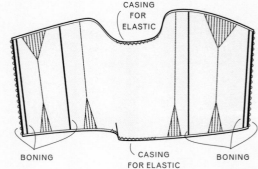

Work third hip dart.

Work 2 rows in Garter st.

[Change to MC and work 6 rows in St st, then change to CC and work 2 rows in Garter st] twice.

Work second bust dart.

Work fourth hip dart.

Work 2 rows in Garter st.

Change to MC and work 6 rows in St st.

Change to CC and work 2 rows in Garter st.

Change to MC and work 2 (6, 10, 14) rows in St st.

Work 6 rows in Garter st. BO.

FINISHING

Using smaller needles and MC, pick up and knit 3 sts for every 4 rows along lower edge of corset. Knit 1 row. Change to CC and knit 2 rows. Change to MC, knit 1 row, then BO. Repeat at top edge of corset.

Using yarn needle and MC, embroider a row of V's (see Special Techniques—Casing for Elastic) between safety pins at upper back edge of corset to make casing for elastic, making sure embroidery is invisible on outside. Cut elastic to desired length, and weave through casing. Using sewing needle and thread, secure ends of elastic. Repeat for lower back edge of corset.

Cut hook-and-eye tape to 13½ (13½, 14½, 14½)". Separate halves of hook-and-eye tape. Fold each half lengthwise with WS together, and machine-sew long edges closed. Cut two pieces of boning to 12½ (12½, 13½, 13½)" and insert into hook-and-eye tape casings. Fold over ends of casings, and sew shut. Hand-baste casings to fronts, and hand- or machine-sew firmly.

Cut four pieces of channeling to 13½ (13½, 14½, 14½)". Cut four pieces of boning to 12½ (12½, 13½, 13½)" and insert into channeling. Fold over ends of channeling, and sew shut. Apply to inside of corset as shown in illustration.

CORSET-BODICE NIGHTGOWN

What could be sweeter to sleep in than a hand-stitched nightie? Loosely knit out of a linen yarn and sewn to a fabric skirt, my version is soft, cool on summer nights, and very romantic.

Simple-to-work lace decorates the off-the-shoulder sleeves and hip, and vertical ladder-stitch columns recall the boned ribbing of the corset, but with none of the constriction. It is shown here over a flouncy petticoat for still more girly appeal. Alternatively, leave the skirt off completely for a lacy top to layer over a tank and jeans.

FINISHED MEASUREMENTS
31½ (34, 37, 39 ½, 42, 45, 47 ½, 50)" chest
13 (13, 13 ½, 14, 14, 14 ½, 15, 15)" length to armhole at
   side seam, not including lace trim
Nightgown shown measures 31½" at chest

YARN
Louet Sales Euroflax sport weight (100% linen; 270 yards /
   100 grams): 2 (3, 3, 4, 4, 5, 5, 6) skeins color champagne

NEEDLES
One pair straight needles size US 7 (4.5 mm)
Change needle size if necessary to obtain correct gauge.

NOTIONS
Yarn needle
Steam iron
Sewing pins
1½ yards ¼" elastic
Sewing needle and thread
2 ¼ yards 54", 58", or 60" wide sheer woven fabric
Fabric scissors
Sewing machine

GAUGE
18 sts and 24 rows = 4" (10 cm) in Stockinette stitch
   (St st)

BACK

CO 71 (77, 83, 89, 95, 101, 107, 113) sts, and work even in St st for 1".

Shape Waist: Decrease 1 st at each end of needle every 4 rows 4 times—63 (69, 75, 81, 87, 93, 99, 105) sts.

Work even for 1 (1, 1½, 1½, 2, 2, 2, 2)".

Increase 1 st at each end of needle every 6 rows 4 times—71 (77, 83, 89, 95, 101, 107, 113) sts.

Work even until Back measures 13 (13, 13½, 14, 14, 14½, 15, 15)".

Shape Armholes: BO 3 (5, 8, 8, 7, 7, 8, 8) sts at beginning of next two rows and 3 (2, 3, 3, 5, 6, 8, 8) sts at the beginning of following two rows, then decrease 1 st at each end of needle every other row 1 (3, 2, 1, 3, 3, 3, 4) times—57 (57, 57, 65, 65, 69, 69, 73) sts remain.

Work even until armholes measure 2 (2, 3, 3, 3½, 3½, 4, 4)". BO.

FRONT

CO 15 sts, and follow chart A, casting on 4 sts at the ends of rows 2 through 11, then casting on 8 (11, 14, 17, 20, 23, 26, 29) sts at the ends of rows 12 and 13—71 (77, 83, 89, 95, 101, 107, 113) sts.

Continuing in pattern established on rows 15 and 16, work even Front measures 1" at side seam.

Shape Waist: Decrease 1 st at each end of needle every 4 rows 4 times—63 (69, 75, 81, 87, 93, 99, 105) sts.

Work even for 1 (1, 1½, 1½, 2, 2, 2, 2)".

Increase 1 st at each end of needle every 6 rows 4 times—71 (77, 83, 89, 95, 101, 107, 113) sts.

Work even until Front measures same as Back along side seam.

Shape Armholes: Work same as for Back.

LACE FOR NECKLINE/SLEEVES

CO 16 sts. Work chart B 17 (17, 17, 18, 18, 18, 19, 19) times. BO.

LACE FOR HIP

CO 16 sts. Work chart B 18 (18, 18, 19, 19, 19, 20, 20) times. BO.

FINISHING

Assemble Bodice: Sew side seams.

Attach Lace: Steam-press both pieces of lace to open up lace.

Sew ends of Neckline/Sleeve lace together to form circle. Place seam at upper center back of bodice and pin in place. Pin lace at center front of bodice as shown in photo. Sew lace to top edge of front and back of bodice.

Sew ends of Hip lace together to form circle. Place seam at lower center back of bodice and pin in place. Pin lace at center front as shown in photo. Sew lace to bottom edge of bodice.

Add Elastic: Using yarn needle and yarn, embroider a row of V's (see Special Techniques—Casing for Elastic) on inside of top edge of bodice to make casing for elastic. Cut elastic to desired length, and thread through casing. Using sewing needle and thread, secure ends of elastic.

Assemble Skirt: Lay out fabric and cut out front and back as shown in step 1.

Sew right sides together at side seams as shown in step 2. Press side seams open.

Pleat skirt as shown in step 3, pinning each pleat in place. Try skirt on dress form or the intended recipient, pinning top of skirt to fit waist area closely.

Assemble Dress: Put bodice on over skirt, and smooth down over pleats. Arrange pleats in a pleasing fashion, and pin bodice to skirt. Machine-sew bodice to skirt using two lines of straight stitching. Trim away excess fabric at inside waist of skirt.

Hem bottom of nightgown. Press lightly.

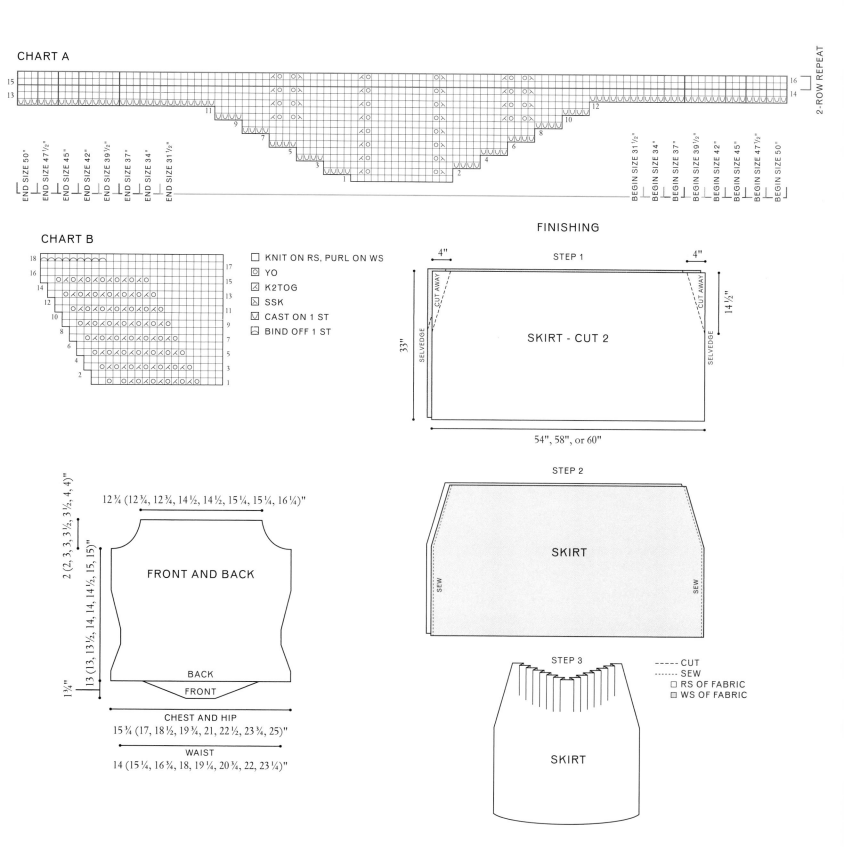

CHART A

15
13

2-ROW REPEAT
16
14

END SIZE 50"
END SIZE 47½"
END SIZE 45"
END SIZE 42"
END SIZE 39½"
END SIZE 37"
END SIZE 34"
END SIZE 31½"

11
9
7
5
3
1

2
4
6
8
10
12

BEGIN SIZE 31½"
BEGIN SIZE 34"
BEGIN SIZE 37"
BEGIN SIZE 39½"
BEGIN SIZE 42"
BEGIN SIZE 45"
BEGIN SIZE 47½"
BEGIN SIZE 50"

CHART B

18
16
14
12
10
8
6
4
2

17
15
13
11
9
7
5
3
1

☐ KNIT ON RS, PURL ON WS
◉ YO
⊠ K2TOG
⊠ SSK
☐ CAST ON 1 ST
☐ BIND OFF 1 ST

FRONT AND BACK

12 ¾ (12 ¾, 12 ¾, 14 ½, 14 ½, 15 ¼, 15 ¼, 16 ¼)"

2 (2, 3, 3, 3 ½, 3 ½, 4, 4)"

13 (13, 13 ½, 14, 14, 14 ½, 15, 15)"

1 ¾"

BACK
FRONT

CHEST AND HIP
15 ¾ (17, 18 ½, 19 ¾, 21, 22 ½, 23 ¾, 25)"

WAIST
14 (15 ¼, 16 ¾, 18, 19 ¼, 20 ¾, 22, 23 ¼)"

FINISHING

STEP 1

4"
4"

CUT AWAY
CUT AWAY

SELVEDGE
SELVEDGE

33"
14 ½"

SKIRT - CUT 2

54", 58", or 60"

STEP 2

SKIRT

SEW
SEW

STEP 3

SKIRT

- - - - CUT
· · · · · SEW
☐ RS OF FABRIC
☐ WS OF FABRIC

EMBOSSED LEAF AND CABLE MERRY WIDOW SHELL

The first merry widow was created by the lingerie company Maidenform to coincide with the release of the 1952 film The Merry Widow, *starring Lana Turner. The original garment was a full-length, strapless corselette with half-cups on top and long garters below. It relied upon steel boning, underwires, and elastic net for shaping, reputedly prompting Turner herself to comment, "The merry widow was designed by a man. A woman would never do that to another woman."*

My merry-widow–inspired shell is infinitely more comfortable but still as shapely, thanks to interior darts, gentle side shaping, and a flattering mock cable and leaf pattern that winds its way from top to bottom on both sides. The boning of the 1950s merry widow was encased in channeling that was held in place by stitching visible from the outside of the garment, a subtle detail that emphasized a woman's curves. While sleeve straps eliminate the need for boning in my version, I've duplicated this subtle detail with traveling cables.

FINISHED MEASUREMENTS
33 (35 ½, 38 ½, 41 ½, 45)" chest
28 ½ (31, 34, 37, 40 ½)" waist
34 ½ (37, 39 ½, 42 ½, 46)" hip
Shell shown measures 35 ½" at chest

YARN
Louet Sales Gems sport weight (100% merino wool; 225
   yards / 100 grams): 3 (3, 4, 4, 5) skeins #80.2853 robin

NEEDLES
One pair straight needles size US 6 (4 mm)
Change needle size if necessary to obtain correct gauge.

NOTIONS
Yarn needle
Crochet hook size US F/5 (3.75 mm)

GAUGE
22 sts and 32 rows = 4" (10 cm) in Stockinette stitch
   (St st)

Pay careful attention when following this shell's charts. To reduce clutter:

• Blank squares represent stitches to be purled on the right side and knit on the wrong side.

• Squares with vertical bars represent stitches to be knit on the right side and purled on the wrong side.

• Dart shaping is shown via "no stitch" symbols only. Decrease each time a dart widens by another "no stitch" symbol; increase each time a dart narrows by a "no stitch" symbol.

• Shaping at selvedges is shown via outlines only. Increase multiple stitches by casting on at the end of a row. Decrease multiple stitches by binding off at the beginning of a row. Increase or decrease by a single stitch at the beginning or end of a right-side row.

• Each embossed leaf is indicated on the Back and Front charts by a series of squares numbered 1 through 16. Refer to the key or to the Embossed Leaf chart for detailed instructions.

• Seven mock cables are shown. Work all seven for the largest three sizes, but only the center five for the smallest two sizes.

BACK

CO 95 (103, 109, 117, 127) sts.

Follow chart for desired size through row 40.

Work even in stitch pattern as established for ½ (1 ½, 2, 3, 3 ½)", then continue with chart.

When last row of shoulders is completed, BO.

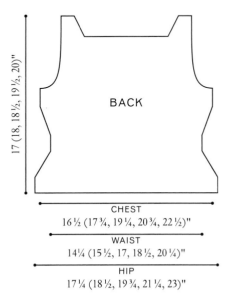

17 (18, 18 ½, 19 ½, 20)"

BACK

CHEST
16 ½ (17 ¾, 19 ¼, 20 ¾, 22 ½)"

WAIST
14 ¼ (15 ½, 17, 18 ½, 20 ¼)"

HIP
17 ¼ (18 ½, 19 ¾, 21 ¼, 23)"

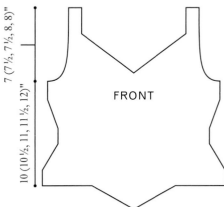

7 (7 ½, 7 ½, 8, 8)"

10 (10 ½, 11, 11 ½, 12)"

FRONT

FRONT

CO 1 st.

Follow chart for desired size through row 58.

Work even in stitch pattern as established for ½ (1½, 2, 3, 3½)", then continue with chart.

When last row of shoulders is completed, BO.

FINISHING

Sew left shoulder seam. Using crochet hook, work one row of single crochet around neck edge, working 1 sc for every st and 3 sc for every 4 rows. Then WITHOUT TURNING, work a second row of single crochet in the opposite direction. Fasten off.

Sew right shoulder seam. Work crocheted edge around armholes as for neckline.

Sew left side seam. Work crocheted edge around hem as for neckline. Sew right side seam.

Steam press entire garment lightly, taking care not to flatten leaf motifs.

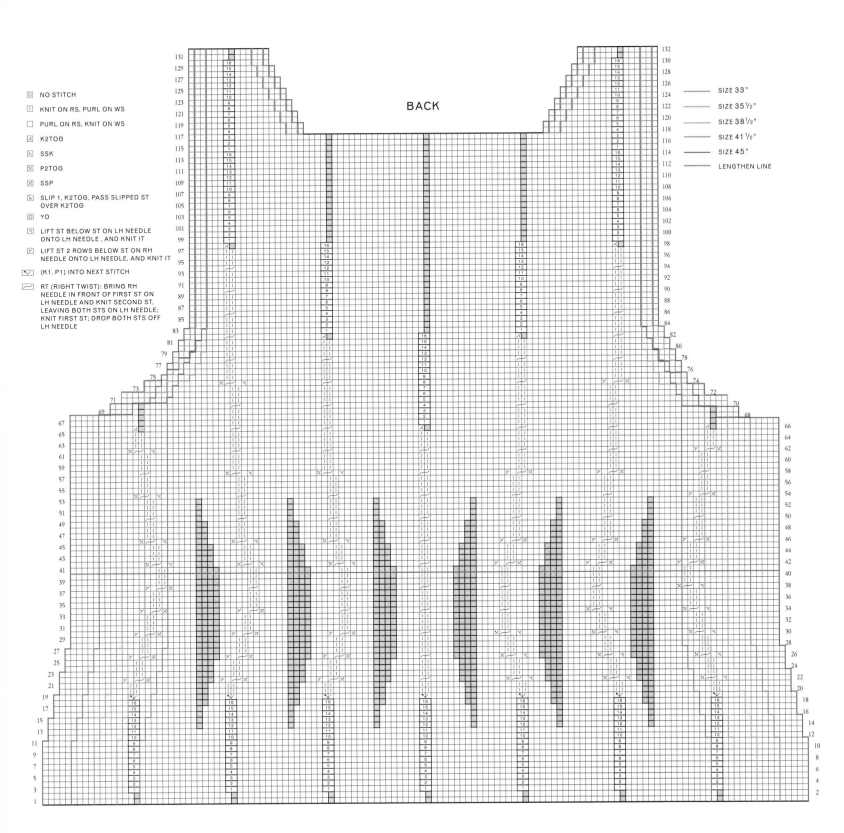

BACK

	SIZE 33"
	SIZE 35½"
	SIZE 38½"
	SIZE 41½"
	SIZE 45"
	LENGTHEN LINE

Legend:

- NO STITCH
- KNIT ON RS, PURL ON WS
- PURL ON RS, KNIT ON WS
- K2TOG
- SSK
- P2TOG
- SSP
- SLIP 1, K2TOG, PASS SLIPPED ST OVER K2TOG
- YO
- LIFT ST BELOW ST ON LH NEEDLE, AND KNIT IT
- LIFT ST 2 ROWS BELOW ST ON RH NEEDLE ONTO LH NEEDLE, AND KNIT IT
- (K1, P1) INTO NEXT STITCH
- RT (RIGHT TWIST): BRING RH NEEDLE IN FRONT OF FIRST ST ON LH NEEDLE AND KNIT SECOND ST, LEAVING BOTH STS ON LH NEEDLE; KNIT FIRST ST; DROP BOTH STS OFF LH NEEDLE

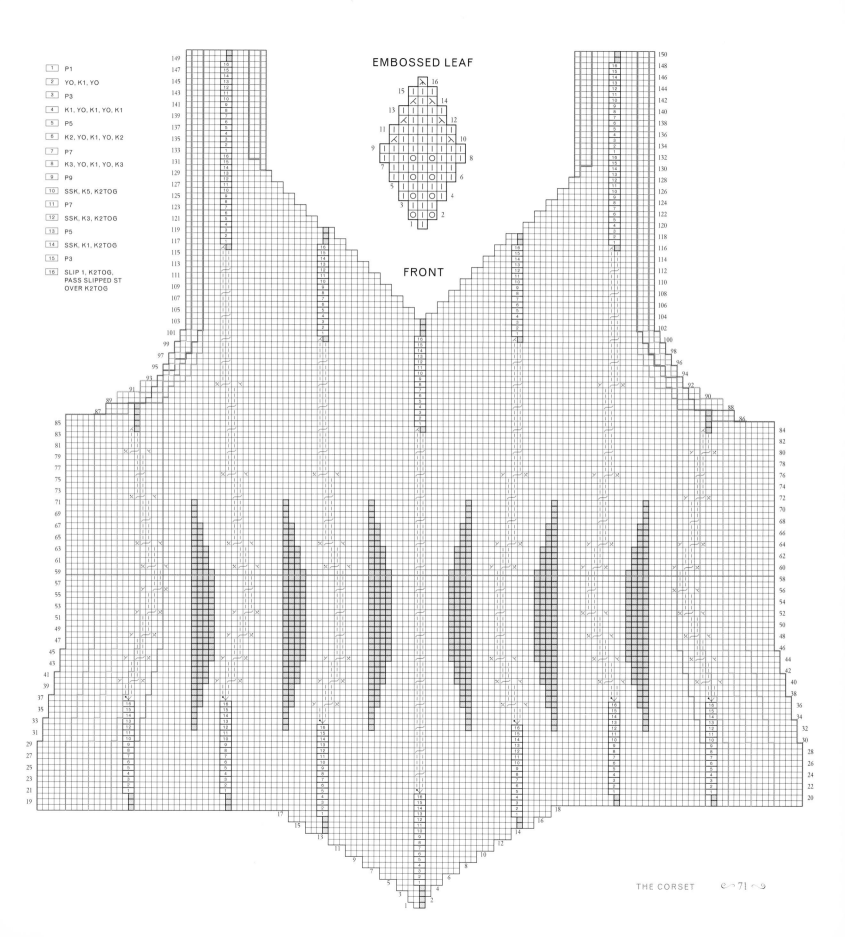

P1

YO, K1, YO

P3

K1, YO, K1, YO, K1

P5

K2, YO, K1, YO, K2

P7

K3, YO, K1, YO, K3

P9

SSK, K5, K2TOG

P7

SSK, K3, K2TOG

P5

SSK, K1, K2TOG

P3

SLIP 1, K2TOG, PASS SLIPPED ST OVER K2TOG

EMBOSSED LEAF

FRONT

FEATHER-TRIMMED CABLED BUSTIER AND FINGERLESS GLOVES

In 17th-century England, Puritans saw corsetry not as a high fashion ideal, but as a way to further the concepts of rigidity, self-discipline, and conformity. Nothing could be further from the purpose of this sultry corset-inspired set. Worked in a buttery-soft Tencel/alpaca yarn in a fiery red, it is anything but puritanical.

The typical bustier covers the torso from the natural waist to the bust. It may or may not have underwiring, but it does feature boning and is usually strapless with a bare back. In this version, I've added straps for support, but the body-baring qualities are left quite intact. The slanting cables in this ensemble nip the waistline and add a vertical line, and flirty feather trim highlights feminine assets. Clever interior shaping brings cables to a V-shaped point at the lower front, quite reminiscent of 1950s corselettes. Add a pair of matching long fingerless gloves, and you're ready to go.

SIZES
Bustier: To fit 33 (36, 40)" chest

FINISHED MEASUREMENTS
Gloves: 16 ½" long from bicep to knuckles; 12" around
   bicep
Bustier shown fits 33" chest

YARN
Classic Elite Miracle (50% alpaca / 50% Tencel;
   108 yards / 50 grams)
   Bustier: 3 (3, 4) skeins #3358 chalet red
   Gloves: 2 skeins #3358 chalet red

NEEDLES
One pair straight needles size US 6 (4 mm)
Change needle size if necessary to obtain correct gauge.

NOTIONS
Stitch markers
Cable needle
Yarn needle
Sewing needle and thread
30" feather trim
½ yard 1" satin ribbon

GAUGE
24 sts and 26 rows = 4" (10 cm) in Stockinette stitch
   (St st)

BUSTIER FRONT

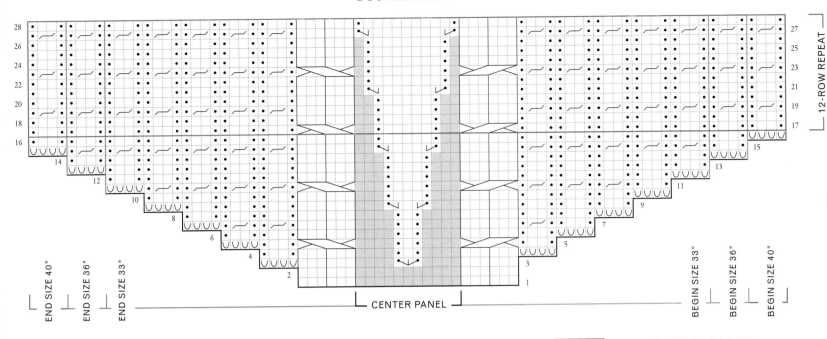

12-ROW REPEAT

CENTER PANEL

END SIZE 40" END SIZE 36" END SIZE 33"

BEGIN SIZE 33" BEGIN SIZE 36" BEGIN SIZE 40"

MINI MOCK CABLE

4-ST REPEAT

☐ KNIT ON RS, PURL ON WS

· PURL ON RS, KNIT ON WS

LIFT STRAND BETWEEN NEEDLES AND (P1, K1, P1) INTO STRAND

(P1, K1) INTO NEXT STITCH

(K1, P1) INTO NEXT STITCH

RT (RIGHT TWIST): BRING RIGHT-HAND NEEDLE IN FRONT OF FIRST ST ON LEFT-HAND NEEDLE AND KNIT SECOND ST, LEAVING BOTH STS ON LEFT-HAND NEEDLE; KNIT FIRST ST; DROP BOTH STS OFF LEFT-HAND NEEDLE

SLIP NEXT 3 STS TO CN, HOLD TO BACK, K3, K3 FROM CN

SLIP NEXT 3 STS TO CN, HOLD TO FRONT, K3, K3 FROM CN

☑ CAST ON 1 ST

☐ NO STITCH

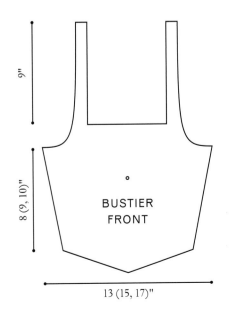

9"

8 (9, 10)"

BUSTIER FRONT

13 (15, 17)"

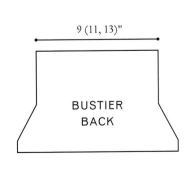

9 (11, 13)"

BUSTIER BACK

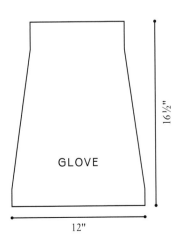

16½"

GLOVE

12"

STITCH PATTERNS

Mini Mock Cable

(multiple of 4 sts + 2; 4-row repeat) (See Chart)

Row 1 (RS): P2, *k2, p2, repeat from *.

Rows 2 and 4: K2, *p2, k2, repeat from *.

Row 3: P2, *RT, p2, repeat from *.

Repeat Rows 1-4 for Mini Mock Cable.

BUSTIER FRONT

CO 12 sts. Work first 2 rows of chart.

Row 3 (RS): Work across 6 sts, pm, with tip of RH needle lift strand between needles, (p1, k1, p1) into strand, pm, work across 6 sts, CO 4 sts—19 sts.

Continue to work according to chart, using cabled CO method (see Special Techniques—Cabled CO) to CO 4 sts at end of every row a total of 10 (12, 14) times and increasing 2 sts in center section every 6 rows as indicated until center panel contains 19 sts between markers 71 (79, 87) sts.

Next RS row: Work to first marker, sm, p1, k8, yo, k2tog, work to end.

Continue to work according to chart until center panel contains 25 (27, 29) sts between markers.

Shape Armholes: BO 8 (8, 10) sts at beginning of next 2 rows and 6 (8, 8) sts at beginning of following 2 rows, then decrease 1 st at each end of needle every other row 5 (7, 9) times—7 sts remain outside each marker.

Shape Front Neck and Straps: Next RS row: P1, work across cable, discard marker, p1, BO center Stockinette sts, p1, discard marker, work across cable, p1.

Attach second ball of yarn and work cable straps for 9" or desired length. BO.

BUSTIER BACK

CO 98 (106, 114) sts.

Work in p2, k2 rib beginning and ending with p2 until Back measures 1" from beginning.

Shape Sides: Decrease 1 st at each end of needle every 4 rows 13 times—72 (80, 88) sts.

Continue to work evenly until Back measures same as Front to armhole shaping at side seam. BO in rib.

FINISHING

Steam all pieces lightly, taking care not to stretch ribbing or cables.

Using yarn needle and yarn, sew Front to Back at side seams. Sew together bottoms of center front cables to form point. Sew strap ends together at back of neck.

Using sewing needle and thread, sew feather trim onto Front as shown in photo.

Gather center front at bust with satin ribbon and tie ribbon into bow.

GLOVES (make 2)

CO 62 sts and work in p2, k2 rib for 4 rows.

Change to Mini Mock Cable and work for 10 rows.

Shape Arm: Decrease 1 st at each end of needle every 10 rows 8 times—46 sts remain.

Continuing in pattern, work even until glove measures 16" from beginning; end ready to work RS row.

Change to p2, k2 rib and and work even for ½". BO.

FINISHING

Steam gloves lightly, taking care not to stretch ribbing or cables.

Using yarn needle and yarn, sew glove seams.

Using sewing needle and thread, sew feather trim around top of glove.

WAIST-CINCHER TOP

The waist cincher, or "waspie," was still another modified corsetlike garment popular in the late 1950s, helpful in achieving the wasp waist of Dior's New Look. It was essentially a wide, elasticized, and boned belt that cinched the midriff, waist, and upper hips, often with garters to hold up stockings.

I've taken the detailing of the waspie and applied it to my Waist-Cincher Top, adding a bodice and sleeves to a slimming midriff section. Ladder stitching keeps the eye moving up and down the waist and is repeated in the sleeves, while the deep surplice bodice adds more figure flattery.

FINISHED MEASUREMENTS
34 (38, 42, 46, 50, 54)" chest
20 ½ (21, 22 ½, 23, 24 ½, 25)" length from shoulder to
  hem
Top shown measures 34" at chest

YARN
Classic Elite Lush (50% angora / 50% wool; 123 yards /
  50 grams): 6 (7, 7, 8, 8, 9) skeins #4419 pink icing (MC)
Berroco Zen Colors (55% cotton / 45% nylon; 110 yards /
  50 grams): 1 skein #8115 Toyko rose (CC)

NEEDLES
One pair straight needles size US 7 (4.5 mm)
One pair straight needles size US 5 (3.75 mm)
Change needle size if necessary to obtain correct gauge.

NOTIONS
Stitch marker
Stitch holder
Yarn needle

GAUGE
18 sts and 24 rows = 4" (10 cm) in Stockinette stitch
  (St st) using larger needles

STITCH PATTERN

Lace Pattern

(multiple of 9 sts + 4; 2-row repeat) (See Chart)

Row 1 (RS): *K4, k2tog, yo, k1, yo, ssk, repeat from *, end k4.

Row 2: Purl.

Repeat Rows 1-2 for Lace Pattern.

BACK

Using CC and larger needles, CO 76 (85, 94, 103, 112, 121) sts.

[Using CC, knit 2 rows. Using MC, work 2 repeats of Lace Pattern] 3 times.

Using MC, continue in Lace Pattern until Back measures 4 (4, 4½, 4½, 5, 5)" from beginning.

Change to smaller needles and continue in Lace Pattern until Back measures 11" from beginning.

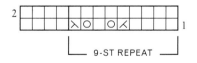

9-ST REPEAT

☐ KNIT ON RS, PURL ON WS   ⟋ K2TOG

☐ YO   ⟍ SSK

Change to larger needles and work even in St st until Back measures 14 (14, 15, 15, 16, 16)" from beginning.

Shape Armholes: BO 4 (4, 6, 7, 8, 11) sts at beginning of next two rows and 3 (3, 4, 4, 5, 6) sts at beginning of following two rows—62 (71, 74, 81, 86, 87) sts.

Decrease 1 st at each end of needle every other row 2 (4, 3, 5, 4, 3) times—58 (63, 68, 71, 78, 81) sts.

Continuing in St st, work even until armholes measure 6½ (7, 7½, 8, 8½, 9)" from first armhole BO.

Shape Shoulders: BO 6 (6, 6, 6, 8, 8) sts at beginning of next four rows and 7 (7, 8, 8, 9, 10) sts at beginning of next two rows. BO remaining 20 (25, 28, 31, 28, 29) sts.

FRONT

Work as for Back until Front measures 11" from beginning, ending ready to work a RS row.

Change to larger needles, knit across 23 (27, 31, 32, 34, 36) sts, pm, knit 30 (31, 32, 39, 44, 49) sts—53 (58, 63, 71, 78, 85) sts in left front. Place remaining 23 (27, 31, 32, 34, 36) sts on holder for right front.

Shape Left Front: Working in St st, (yo, ssk) after marker on every RS row 5 times to create faux bust dart and AT THE SAME TIME shape neck as follows: BO 3 (3, 3, 4, 4, 4) sts at beginning of every WS row 5 (5, 5, 4, 5, 5) times, then BO 2

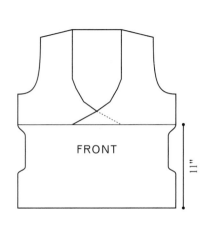

FRONT

11"

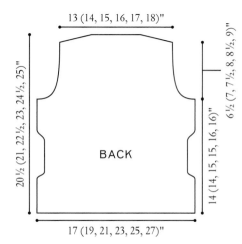

13 (14, 15, 16, 17, 18)"

6½ (7, 7½, 8, 8½, 9)"

20½ (21, 22½, 23, 24½, 25)"

14 (14, 15, 15, 16, 16)"

BACK

17 (19, 21, 23, 25, 27)"

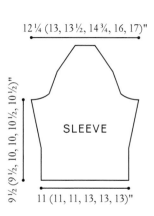

12¼ (13, 13½, 14¾, 16, 17)"

9½ (9½, 10, 10, 10½, 10½)"

SLEEVE

11 (11, 11, 13, 13, 13)"

sts at beginning of every WS row 2 (4, 4, 5, 5, 6) times, then decrease 1 st at beginning of every WS row 4 (3, 5, 7, 4, 5) times, then decrease 1 st at beginning of every other WS row 2 times. AT THE SAME TIME, continuing neck shaping, when left front measures same as Back at side seam, shape armhole as for Back.

Work even until left front measures same as Back at armhole.

Shape shoulder as for Back.

Shape Right Front: Slip sts from holder to larger needles.

With WS facing, purl across 23 (27, 31, 32, 34, 36) sts, pm, and CO 30 (31, 32, 39, 44, 49) sts—53 (58, 63, 71, 78, 85) sts in right front.

Working in St st, (yo, ssk) after marker on every RS row 5 times to create faux bust dart and AT THE SAME TIME shape neck as follows: BO 3 (3, 3, 4, 4, 4) sts at beginning of every RS row 5 (5, 5, 4, 5, 5) times, then BO 2 sts at beginning of every RS row 2 (4, 4, 5, 5, 6) times, then decrease 1 st at beginning of every RS row 4 (3, 5, 7, 4, 5) times, then decrease 1 st at beginning of every other RS row 2 times. AT THE SAME TIME, continuing neck shaping, when right front measures same as Back at side seam, shape armhole as for Back.

Work even until right front measures same as Back at armhole.

Shape shoulder as for Back.

SLEEVES (make 2)

Using CC and larger needles, CO 49 (49, 49, 58, 58, 58) sts and work as for Back until Sleeve measures 4" from beginning.

Increase 1 st at each end of needle every 6 (6, 6, 6, 4, 4) rows 3 (5, 6, 4, 7, 9) times—55 (59, 61, 66, 72, 76) sts.

Continuing in Lace Pattern, work even until Sleeve measures 9½ (9½, 10, 10, 10½, 10½)" from beginning, ending ready to work a RS row.

BO 4 (4, 6, 9, 8, 11) sts at beginning of next 2 rows and 3 (4, 4, 5, 6, 6) sts at beginning of following 2 rows—41 (43, 41, 38, 44, 42) sts.

Decrease 1 st at each end of needle every 4 rows 3 (3, 4, 4, 6) times, then every other row 10 (11, 10, 10, 11, 9) times—15 (15, 13, 10, 14, 12) sts.

BO remaining sts.

FINISHING

Sew side and shoulder seams.

Using smaller needles and CC, and with RS facing, pick up and knit 3 sts for every 4 rows and 1 st for every st along right front neck edge, back neck edge, and left front neck edge. Knit 1 row, then BO.

Tuck right surplice neckline edge to inside, and slip-stitch invisibly to bodice front.

Sew underarm seams, and set in sleeves.

Press entire garment lightly, steaming open lace.

LACED-FRONT SWEATER

Ribbed boning and lacing were two of the more memorable components of traditional corsetry. Just those two details alone add sexy simplicity to this pretty sweater. Ribbing mimics the look of boning in a close-fitting but comfortable way, and lacing shapes the cardigan while leaving just enough to the imagination. Sparkly lamé in the wool/silk blend yarn twinkles with glamour day or night. Layer this sleek sweater over a tank or wear it over bare skin.

SIZES
To fit 32 (35, 38, 41, 44, 47)" chest

FINISHED MEASUREMENTS
28 (30 ½, 33, 36, 38 ½, 41)" chest
21 (21 ½, 22 ½, 23, 24, 24 ½)" length from shoulder
   to hem
16 ½ (17, 17, 17 ½, 18, 18)" sleeve length
Sample shown measures 28" at chest

YARN
Diakeito Diacouture Silklame (58% wool / 40% silk /
   2% polyester; 126 yards / 40 grams): 8 (8, 9, 9, 10, 10)
   balls #903 lilac

NEEDLES
One pair straight needles size US 6 (4 mm)
One pair double-pointed needles size US 6 (4 mm)
Change needle size if necessary to obtain correct gauge.

NOTIONS
Yarn needle
Crochet hook size US G/6 (4 mm)
2 decorative beads, for end of I-cord laces

GAUGE
24 sts and 32 rows = 4" (10 cm) in ribbed pattern,
   unstretched, after blocking

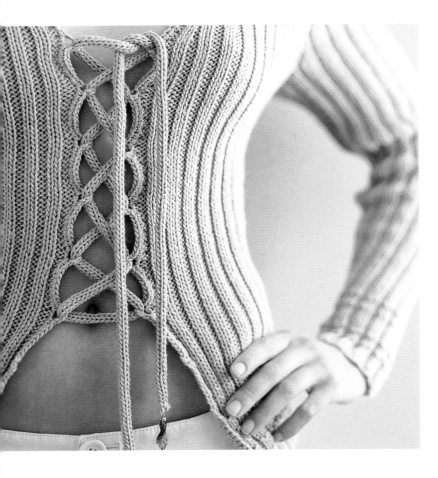

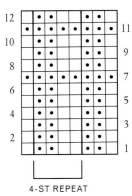

4-ST REPEAT

☐ KNIT ON RS, PURL ON WS

☑ PURL ON RS, KNIT ON WS

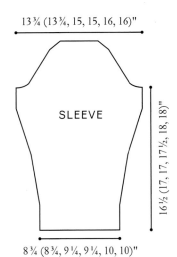

SLEEVE

13 ¾ (13 ¾, 15, 15, 16, 16)"

16 ½ (17, 17, 17 ½, 18, 18)"

8 ¾ (8 ¾, 9 ¼, 9 ¼, 10, 10)"

NOTES

Keep first and last st of each row (the selvedge sts) in Stockinette st. Work increases and decreases inside selvedge sts.

STITCH PATTERN

Interrupted Rib Pattern
(multiple of 4 sts; 12-row repeat) (See Chart)

Rows 1, 3, 5, and 9 (RS): K1, p2, *k2, p2; repeat from * to last st, end k1.

Rows 2, 4, 6, 8, 10, and 12: P1, *k2, p2; repeat from * to last 3 sts, end k2, p1.

Rows 7 and 11: Purl.

Repeat Rows 1–12 for Interrupted Rib Pattern.

To work k2, p2 rib after Interrupted Rib, k all k sts and p all p sts.

BACK

CO 78 (86, 94, 102, 110, 118) sts.

Working 1 selvedge st at each end of needle, work center 76 (84, 92, 100, 108, 116) sts in Interrupted Rib Pattern.

Work through row 12 of pattern 2 times, then work in k2, p2 rib until Back measures 6 ½ (7, 7 ½, 8, 8 ½, 9)" from beginning.

Increase 1 st at each end of needle every 6 rows 4 times, working new sts into k2, p2 rib—86 (94, 102, 110, 118, 126) sts.

Continuing in k2, p2 rib, work even until Back measures 13 ½ (14, 14 ½, 15, 15 ½, 16)" from beginning, ending with a WS row.

Shape Armholes: BO 6 sts at the beginning of next two rows, then BO 0 (0, 3, 4, 5, 6) sts at beginning of following two rows—74 (82, 84, 90, 96, 102) sts remain.

Decrease 1 st at each end of needle every other row 3 times— 68 (76, 78, 84, 90, 96) sts remain. Work even until armholes measure 7 ½ (7 ½, 8, 8, 8 ½, 8 ½)".

Shape Shoulders: Continuing in k2, p2 rib, BO 5 (6, 6, 6, 7, 7) sts at beginning of next 6 rows, then BO 6 (6, 8, 8, 7, 9) sts at beginning of following 2 rows—26 (28, 26, 32, 34, 36) sts remain. BO remaining sts in rib.

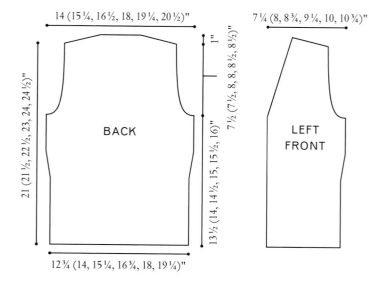

14 (15 ¼, 16 ½, 18, 19 ¼, 20 ½)"

21 (21 ½, 22 ½, 23, 24, 24 ½)"

BACK

12 ¾ (14, 15 ¼, 16 ¾, 18, 19 ¼)"

1"

7 ½ (7 ½, 8, 8, 8 ½, 8 ½)"

13 ½ (14, 14 ½, 15, 15 ½, 16)"

7 ¼ (8, 8 ¾, 9 ¼, 10, 10 ¾)"

LEFT FRONT

RIGHT FRONT

CO 42 (46, 50, 54, 58, 62) sts.

Working 1 selvedge st at each end of needle, work center 40 (44, 48, 52, 56, 60) sts in Interrupted Rib Pattern.

Work through row 12 of pattern 2 times, then work in k2, p2 rib until Front measures 6 ½ (7, 7 ½, 8, 8 ½, 9)" from beginning.

Increase 1 st at side-seam edge of work every 6 rows 4 times, working new sts into k2, p2 rib—46 (50, 54, 58, 62, 66) sts.

Continuing in k2, p2 rib, work even until Front measures same as Back to armhole.

Shape Armhole and Neck: Work armhole as for left side of Back, and AT THE SAME TIME decrease 1 st 5 sts in from neck edge every 2 rows 6 (8, 4, 10, 10, 12) times, then every 4 rows 12 (11, 14, 11, 12, 11) times—19 (22, 24, 24, 26, 28) sts remain.

Work even until armhole measures same as for Back.

Shape Shoulders: Continuing in k2, p2 rib, BO 5 (6, 6, 6, 7, 7) sts at beginning of next 3 WS rows, then BO remaining 4 (4, 6, 6, 5, 7) sts at beginning of following WS row.

LEFT FRONT

Work as for Right Front, reversing all shapings.

SLEEVES (make 2)

CO 54 (54, 58, 58, 62, 62) sts.

Working 1 selvedge st at each end of needle, work center 52 (52, 56, 56, 60, 60) sts in Interrupted Rib Pattern.

Work through row 12 of pattern 2 times.

Work in k2, p2 rib, increasing 1 st at each end of needle every 6 rows 5 (5, 6, 6, 6, 6) times, then every 4 rows 10 (10, 11, 11, 12, 12) times, working new sts into rib pattern—84 (84, 92, 92, 98, 98) sts.

Continuing in k2, p2 rib, work even until Sleeve measures 16 ½ (17, 17, 17 ½, 18, 18)" from beginning, ending with a WS row.

Shape Cap: BO 6 sts at beginning of next 2 rows, then BO 0 (0, 4, 4, 5, 5) sts at beginning of following 2 rows—72 (72, 72, 72, 76, 76) sts remain.

Decrease 1 st at each end of needle every other row 16 times—40 (40, 40, 40, 44, 44) sts remain.

BO 2 sts at beginning of every row 8 times—24 (24, 24, 24, 28, 28) sts remain. BO remaining sts.

FINISHING

Lightly steam-block pieces to measurements, taking care to not flatten ribs.

Sew side, shoulder, and underarm seams. Set in sleeves.

Work 1 row of single crochet around front edges and back neck, making 5 loops of chain 5 crochet on each front edge evenly spaced between bottom of neckline at center front and top of pattern stitch near bottom front.

Work I-cord (see Special Techniques) for 45" or to desired length.

Lace I-cord through crocheted loops in a criss-cross configuration as shown in photo. Sew beads to end of I-cord.

chapter 4

THE CAMISOLE

The camisole holds a central spot in today's fashion parade, frequently peeking out from between the lapels of a blazer or calling for attention atop a pair of jeans, but it was originally the lowest of workhorses in the lingerie drawer.

The very earliest form of the camisole was actually a plain, long muslin chemise worn under expensive corsets and other garments to protect them from perspiration and wear from the body inside. It was particularly important in 15th-century Europe, when outer garments for the upper class were made of very expensive fabrics, and bathing was indulged perhaps once every few months. Sachets or fresh flowers were tucked into the chemise between the breasts in an attempt to mask body odors, a custom often remembered on modern lingerie with tiny ribbon roses sewn in the space between the bosoms.

The Victorian era and its new emphasis on cleanliness led to the frequent changing of undergarments and, consequently, the refinement of the garments themselves. During the mid-19th century, with the appearance of pantlike undergarments known as drawers, the chemise was shortened to fit just around the midsection and took on the name camisole. With the abandonment of the corset in the early 1900s, camisoles were suddenly the perfect thing to wear under sheer dresses, and they were profusely decorated with lace, ribbons, and embroidery. The camisole continued to line sheer tops until the 1970s, when hippies who were rediscovering petticoats as skirts also began pulling camisoles and corset covers out of Grandma's trunks and mixing them with jeans and miniskirts.

The camisole has never really gone back undercover. It is now a layering piece and a garment in its own right, and knitted camisoles, in particular, offer countless opportunities for creativity, as the designs in this chapter illustrate. The Silk and Pearls Cami is so easy it can be finished in a weekend, and so elegant it could be worn to a wedding. The Shaped Lace Tee is a lovely way to lend femininity to an outfit without getting frilly, and it's an excellent introduction to lace knitting. The Ruched Camisole can take a daring girl out dancing while showing off her knitting prowess, and the Tank with 3-D Crochet Embellishments looks just as wonderful with jeans or shorts as with a more formal ensemble.

BASIC CAMISOLE

Hand-knitting is ideal for today's camisole. The shape is simple, usually achieved by creating two gently curved rectangles for a front and back, and lends itself easily to styling details like lace insets or trim or appliquéd flowers. Sleeve shaping is simple, ranging from spaghetti straps to more substantial tank-style straps to cap sleeves. Because of its small size, a camisole doesn't require a lot of yarn, so is often a sensible way to indulge in expensive luxury fibers like silk and cashmere.

This raw silk camisole is reminiscent of the knitted vests worn under clothing for warmth during Victorian times. It features a simple but decorative rib stitch and a contrasting lace collar that is knit separately and sewn on. Here, the camisole is shown with a blouse underneath. It would look equally good on its own or peeking out from under a jacket.

FINISHED MEASUREMENTS
31½ (34, 37, 39½, 42, 45, 47½, 50)" chest
13 (13, 13½, 14, 14, 14½, 15, 15)" length to armhole
Camisole shown measures 34" at chest

YARN
Reynolds Mandalay (100% silk; 98 yards / 50 grams):
 5 (5, 6, 6, 7, 7, 8, 8) skeins #39 (MC), 1 skein #11 (CC)

NEEDLES
One pair straight needles size US 10 (6 mm)
One pair straight needles size US 6 (4 mm)
One pair straight needles size US 4 (3.5 mm)
Change needle size if necessary to obtain correct gauge.

NOTIONS
Yarn needle
3 (3, 4, 4, 5, 5, 6, 6) yards elastic thread

GAUGE
18 sts and 24 rows = 4" (10 cm) in Wide Rib on size US 6
 (4 mm) needles

STITCH PATTERNS

Wide Rib

(multiple of 6 sts + 5; 2-row repeat)

Row 1 (RS): *P5, k1, repeat from *, end p5.

Row 2: *K5, p1, repeat from *, end k5.

Repeat Rows 1-2 for Wide Rib.

Lace Pattern

(multiple of 12 sts + 1; 2-row repeat) (See Chart)

Row 1 (RS): K1, *[k2tog] twice, [yo, k1] 3 times, yo, [ssk] twice, k1, repeat from *.

Row 2: Purl.

Repeat Rows 1-2 for Lace Pattern.

BACK

Using MC and size US 6 (4 mm) needles, CO 71 (77, 83, 89, 95, 101, 107, 113) sts.

Work in Wide Rib for 3 (3, 4, 4, 5, 5, 6, 6)".

Change to size US 4 (3.5 mm) needles. Continuing in Wide Rib, work even for 3".

Change to size US 6 (4 mm) needles. Continuing in Wide Rib, work even until Back measures 13 (13, 13 ½, 14, 14, 14 ½, 15, 15)".

Shape Armholes: BO 3 (5, 8, 8, 7, 7, 8, 8) sts at beginning of next two rows and 3 (2, 3, 3, 5, 6, 8, 8) sts at the beginning of following two rows, then decrease 1 st at each end of needle every other row 1 (3, 2, 1, 3, 3, 3, 4) time(s)—57 (57, 57, 65, 65, 69, 69, 73) sts remain.

Continuing in Wide Rib, work even until armholes measure 4 ½".

Change to size US 4 (3.5 mm) needles and BO all sts firmly.

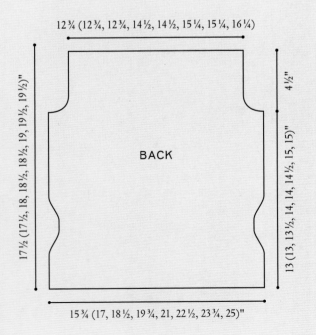

12 ¾ (12 ¾, 12 ¾, 14 ½, 14 ½, 15 ¼, 15 ¼, 16 ¼)"

4 ½"

17 ½ (17 ½, 18, 18 ½, 18 ½, 19, 19 ½, 19 ½)"

13 (13, 13 ½, 14, 14, 14 ½, 15, 15)"

BACK

15 ¾ (17, 18 ½, 19 ¾, 21, 22 ½, 23 ¾, 25)"

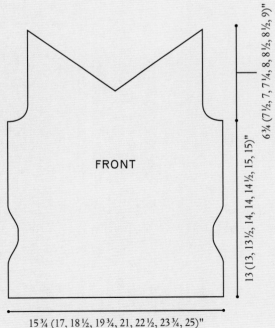

6 ¾ (7 ½, 7, 7 ¼, 8, 8 ½, 8 ½, 9)"

13 (13, 13 ½, 14, 14, 14 ½, 15, 15)"

FRONT

15 ¾ (17, 18 ½, 19 ¾, 21, 22 ½, 23 ¾, 25)"

FRONT

Work as for Back until last armhole decreases have been made.

Continuing in Wide Rib, work even for 1"; end ready to work a RS row.

Shape Neck: With RS facing, work across 28 (28, 28, 32, 32, 34, 34, 36) sts, BO 1 st, work to end—28 (28, 28, 32, 32, 34, 34, 36) sts on each side of neck opening.

Attach second ball of yarn at left neck edge. Working both sides of neck opening simultaneously, BO 2 sts at each neck edge every other row 14 (14, 14, 16, 16, 17, 17, 18) times—0 sts remain.

LACE TRIM (make 2)

Using CC and size US 10 (6 mm) needles, CO 37 sts.

Work Lace Pattern for 1".

Change to size US 6 (4 mm) needles. Continuing in Lace Pattern, work even until lace measures 3" from beginning; end ready to work a WS row.

Change to size US 4 (3.5 mm) needles. With WS facing, purl across. Next row, BO.

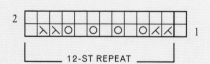

12-ST REPEAT

☐ KNIT ON RS, PURL ON WS   ⟋ K2TOG

☉ YO   ⟍ SSK

FINISHING

Sew side seams.

Armbands and Straps: Using MC and size US 6 (4 mm) needles, CO 20 sts and then with RS facing pick up and knit 3 sts for every 4 rows and 1 st for every bound-off st along right armhole. Work 3 rows of Garter st. BO.

Pick up and knit sts along left armhole as for right, then CO 20 sts. Finish as for right.

Tie on for fit, then sew ends of straps to Back.

Steam-block lace trim, stretching to emphasize lace. Sew to front of camisole, positioning as in photo.

To prevent waistline from stretching out, thread yarn needle with elastic thread and work 4 rows of running stitch ½" apart around inside of waist area. Secure ends.

SHAPED LACE TEE

As undergarments took on more prominence throughout the 19th century, the amount of adornment on them increased—at least on those worn closest to the outside of the body. The corset cover, for example, was usually much more heavily decorated than the camisole worn beneath it, and it often showcased several types of needlework. The particular garment that inspired this lace tee had vertical panels of drawn threadwork running up and down the body, and thickly embroidered floral cutwork at the hem and sleeves.

To mimic the original patterning without needing to work different types of needlework, I chose two different lace stitches. A floral lace pattern trims the hem, sleeves, and flattering square neck, and the vertical lace lines produce a close-fitting, feminine silhouette.

FINISHED MEASUREMENTS
33 ½ (38, 42 ½, 47, 51 ½, 56)" chest
20 (21 ½, 22, 24, 25, 26)" length
Tee shown measures 38" at chest

YARN
Cascade Sierra (80% cotton / 20% wool; 191 yards /
   100 grams): 3 (3, 4, 4, 5, 5) skeins #03 ivory

NEEDLES
One pair straight needles size US 7 (4.5 mm)
One pair straight needles size US 5 (3.75 mm)
Change needle size if necessary to obtain correct gauge.

NOTIONS
Crochet hook size US G/6 (4 mm) for edging
Stitch markers
Yarn needle

GAUGE
16 sts and 24 rows = 4" (10 cm) in stitch pattern B using
   larger needles

STITCH PATTERNS

Stitch pattern A
(Vine Lace, from *A Treasury of Knitting Patterns*
by Barbara G. Walker)
(multiple of 9 sts + 4; 4-row repeat) (See Chart A)

Rows 1 and 3 (WS): Purl.

Row 2: K3, *yo, k2, ssk, k2tog, k2, yo, k1; repeat from *, end k1.

Row 4: K2, *yo, k2, ssk, k2tog, k2, yo, k1; repeat from *, end k2.

Repeat Rows 1-4 for pattern.

Stitch pattern B
(multiple of 9 sts + 4; 2-row repeat) (See Chart B)

Row 1 (RS): *K4, k2tog, yo, k1, yo, ssk; repeat from *, end k4.

Row 2: Purl.

Repeat Rows 1 and 2 for pattern.

BACK

Using larger needles, CO 67 (76, 85, 94, 103, 112) sts loosely.

Work in stitch pattern A for 2 (2, 2 ½, 2 ½, 3, 3)", ending with Row 1 of stitch pattern.

Change to stitch pattern B and work even until Back measures 5 (5, 6, 6, 7, 7)" from beginning.

If waist shaping is desired, change to smaller needles and work waist area even in stitch pattern B for 1½", then change back to larger needles.

Work even in stitch pattern B until Back measures 13 (13, 14½, 16, 16½, 17)".

Shape Armholes: BO 4 (5, 7, 8, 9, 10) sts at beginning of next 2 rows and 3 (4, 6, 7, 8, 8) sts at beginning of following 2 rows.

Decrease 1 st at each end of needle every other row 1 (2, 3, 3, 3, 3) time(s)—51 (54, 53, 58, 63, 70) sts remain.

Work even in stitch pattern B until armholes measure 6 (6 ½, 6 ½, 7, 7 ½, 8)".

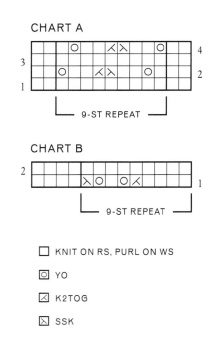

CHART A

3

1

4

2

└─ 9-ST REPEAT ─┘

CHART B

2

1

└─ 9-ST REPEAT ─┘

☐ KNIT ON RS, PURL ON WS

⊡ YO

⊠ K2TOG

⊠ SSK

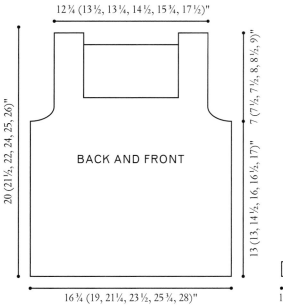

12 ¾ (13 ½, 13 ¼, 14 ½, 15 ¾, 17 ½)"

7 (7 ½, 7 ½, 8, 8 ½, 9)"

20 (21 ½, 22, 24, 25, 26)"

13 (13, 14 ½, 16, 16 ½, 17)"

BACK AND FRONT

16 ¾ (19, 21 ¼, 23 ½, 25 ¾, 28)"

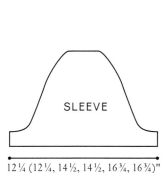

SLEEVE

12 ¼ (12 ¼, 14 ½, 14 ½, 16 ¾, 16 ¾)"

Shape Neck: Work 10 (11, 11, 13, 16, 15) sts, BO next 31 (32, 31, 32, 31, 40) sts, work to end—10 (11, 11, 13, 16, 15) sts in each shoulder.

Attach a second ball of yarn and work both shoulders simultaneously until armholes measure 7 (7 ½, 7 ½, 8, 8 ½, 9)". BO shoulders.

FRONT

Work as for Back until Front measures 13 (13, 14 ½, 16, 16 ½, 17)", ending with a RS row.

Next WS row: P18 (22, 27, 31, 36, 36), pm, p31 (32, 31, 32, 31, 40), pm, p18 (22, 27, 31, 36, 36).

Next RS row: Begin shaping armholes as for Back.

Next WS row: Decrease 0 (1, 0, 1, 0, 0) st(s) evenly across area between markers.

Next RS row: Begin stitch pattern A between markers.

Work even until armholes measure 2 (2, 2, 3, 3, 3)" from beginning, ending with a WS row.

Next RS row: Work across to marker, BO sts between markers, attach a second ball of yarn, and work to end of row.

Work even on both shoulders simultaneously until armholes measure same as for Back.

BO 10 (11, 11, 13, 16, 15) sts at each shoulder.

SLEEVES (make 2)

Using larger needles, CO 49 (49, 58, 58, 67, 67) sts loosely.

Work in stitch pattern A for 1 (1, 1 ½, 2, 2, 3)".

Change to stitch pattern B and work 2 rows.

Continuing in stitch pattern B, BO 4 (5, 7, 8, 9, 10) sts at beginning of next 2 rows and 3 (4, 6, 7, 8, 8) sts at beginning of following 2 rows.

Decrease 1 st at each end of needle every 4 rows 5 (7, 7, 9, 9, 10) times, and 1 st at each end of needle every other row 8 (5, 6, 2, 3, 2) times.

BO remaining 9 (7, 6, 6, 9, 7) sts.

FINISHING

Steam-block all pieces well to open up lace pattern, especially at garment edges.

Sew sides, shoulders, and underarms. Set in sleeves.

Using crochet hook and beginning at center back neck, work 1 round of single crochet around neck edge, working loosely across front lace. Fasten off.

RUCHED CAMISOLE

This sheer camisole with ruched sides is meant to be worn as outerwear, but it requires a layer underneath to preserve the wearer's modesty. If you're daring, what better way to show off a pretty bra? Lace-weight mohair and silk create the sheer, soft fabric for this very modern camisole, but the ribbon rose at the center front is a reminder of the camisole's past—a time when blooms, rather than baths, were depended on to keep the wearer fresh.

SIZES
To fit 31-33 (35-37, 39-41, 43-45)" chest

FINISHED MEASUREMENTS
31 (35, 39, 43)" chest
10 ½ (11, 11½, 12)" length at side seam
Camisole shown fits 31-33" chest

YARN
Knit One, Crochet Too Douceur et Soie (70% baby
    mohair / 30% silk; 225 yards / 25 grams): 2 (2, 3, 3)
    balls #8512

NEEDLES
One pair straight needles size US 9 (5.5 mm)
Change needle size if necessary to obtain correct gauge.

NOTIONS
Yarn needle
1 yard smooth, contrast-color waste yarn
Crochet hook size US G/6 (4 mm)
1 purchased ribbon rose, in matching color
Sewing needle and matching thread

GAUGE
12 sts and 20 rows = 4" (10 cm) in Stockinette st (St st)

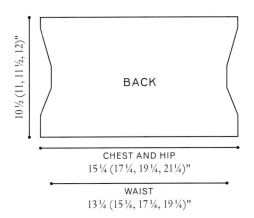

BACK

CHEST AND HIP
15 ¼ (17 ¼, 19 ¼, 21 ¼)"

WAIST
13 ¼ (15 ¼, 17 ¼, 19 ¼)"

10 ½ (11, 11 ½, 12)"

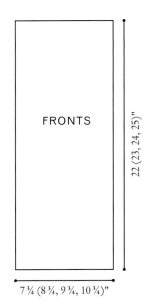

FRONTS

22 (23, 24, 25)"

7 ¾ (8 ¾, 9 ¾, 10 ¾)"

BACK

CO 46 (52, 58, 64) sts loosely.

Work even in St st for 2".

Decrease 1 st at each end of needle every 4 rows 3 times—40 (46, 52, 58) sts. Pm to indicate waist.

Work even for 2".

Increase 1 st at each end of needle every 6 rows 3 times—46 (52, 58, 64) sts.

Work even until Back measures 10 ½ (11, 11 ½, 12)".

BO loosely.

FRONTS (make 2)

CO 23 (26, 29, 32) sts loosely.

Work even in St st for 22 (23, 24, 25)".

BO loosely.

FINISHING

Steam-press all pieces lightly, stretching to measurements on schematic.

Using yarn needle and waste yarn, sew a loose running stitch along side selvedge and cast-on edge of right Front. Gather side selvedge to fit between underarm and waist of Back at side seam, and gather cast-on edge to fit between waist and bottom of Back at side seam. With RS together, sew gathered selvedge to Back from underarm to waist, then swing cast-on edge of right Front vertical with side seam and sew in place from waist to bottom of Back. Remove waste yarn. Repeat with left Front.

Using crochet hook, work edging around all outer edges of camisole as follows:

Rnd 1: *Sc in camisole edge, skip 1 st or 2 rows, ch3, repeat from *, end with sc in 2nd st of 1st ch3 loop.

Rnd 2: *Ch3, sc in 2nd st of next ch3 loop, [ch1, (dc, ch1) 5 times] in next ch3 loop, sc in 2nd st of next ch3 loop, repeat from *.

Fasten off.

Lightly steam edging, spreading out shells.

Using yarn needle and yarn, sew Fronts together invisibly, overlapping 6 of the shells.

Using sewing needle and thread, sew ribbon rose at top center front.

STRAPS (make 2)

Crochet 16 (16, 18, 18)" of chain. Hdc in 3rd ch from hook and each ch across, turn. Ch2, hdc in each hdc across, turn. Fasten off.

Sew to front points. Sew to top of Back, spaced approximately 5" apart.

TANK WITH 3-D CROCHET EMBELLISHMENTS

In this design, the nosegay worn between the breasts in the days of old has been moved to the shoulder, where it embellishes a simple, well-shaped tank. I like to think of it as a juxtaposition of the lowly muslin chemise from which the camisole evolved and a festive corsage.

The flowers, which are crocheted, are stitched on to the camisole here, but they can also be pinned on using jewelry pin backs and then transferred to a hat, jacket, or other garment as desired.

FINISHED MEASUREMENTS
30 ½ (35, 39 ½, 42, 46 ½, 50, 54 ½)" chest
29 (33 ½, 38, 40 ½, 45, 48 ½, 53)" high hip (4"-5" below
   natural waist)
Tank shown measures 30 ½" at chest

YARN
Knit One, Crochet Too Italian Ice (61% cotton /
   26% linen / 13% viscose; 76 yards / 50 grams):
   5 (5, 6, 6, 7, 7, 8) balls #323 mushroom (MC) and
   1 ball each #543 mint (A), #274 strawberry (B),
   #242 guava (C), and #1279 candy (D)

NEEDLES
One pair straight needles size US 9 (5.5 mm)
Change needle size if necessary to obtain correct gauge.

NOTIONS
Yarn needle
Crochet hook size H/8 (5 mm)

GAUGE
18 sts and 24 rows = 4" (10 cm) in Stockinette stitch
   (St st)

BACK

Using MC, CO 65 (75, 85, 91, 101, 109, 119) sts.

Work in St st for 1 (1, 2, 2, 3, 3, 4)".

Shape Waist: Decrease 1 st at each end of needle every 4 rows 4 times—57 (67, 77, 83, 93, 101, 111) sts.

Work even for 4 rows.

Increase 1 st at each end of needle every 4 rows 6 times—69 (79, 89, 95, 105, 113, 123) sts.

Work even until Back measures 12 ¾ (13 ¼, 13 ¾, 14 ¼, 15 ¾, 16 ¾, 17 ¾)" from beginning.

Shape Armholes: BO 4 (4, 5, 7, 9, 10, 10) sts at beginning of next 2 rows, then 3 (4, 4, 6, 7, 8, 9) sts at beginning of following 2 rows—55 (63, 71, 69, 73, 77, 85) sts.

Decrease 1 st at each end of needle every other row 2 (3, 4, 3, 3, 3, 4) times—51 (57, 63, 63, 67, 71, 77) sts.

Work even until armholes measure 6 ¼ (6 ¾, 7 ¾, 7 ¾, 8 ¼, 8 ¾, 9 ¼)" from first underarm bind-off.

Shape Neck: With RS facing, work across 8 (8, 9, 9, 10, 10, 12) sts, BO next 35 (41, 45, 45, 47, 51, 53) sts, work remaining sts—8 (8, 9, 9, 10, 10, 12) sts in each shoulder.

Attach second ball of yarn and continue to work both shoulders simultaneously for ½" more.

BO.

FRONT

Work as for Back until Front measures same as Back to underarms, ending ready to work a RS row.

Next RS row: K34 (39, 44, 47, 52, 56, 61), BO next st, work to end.

Attach a second ball of yarn and, working both shoulders simultaneously, BO 4 (4, 5, 7, 9, 10, 10) sts at each armhole edge, then BO 3 (4, 4, 6, 7, 8, 9) sts at each armhole edge, then decrease 1 st at each armhole edge every other row 2 (3, 4, 3, 3,

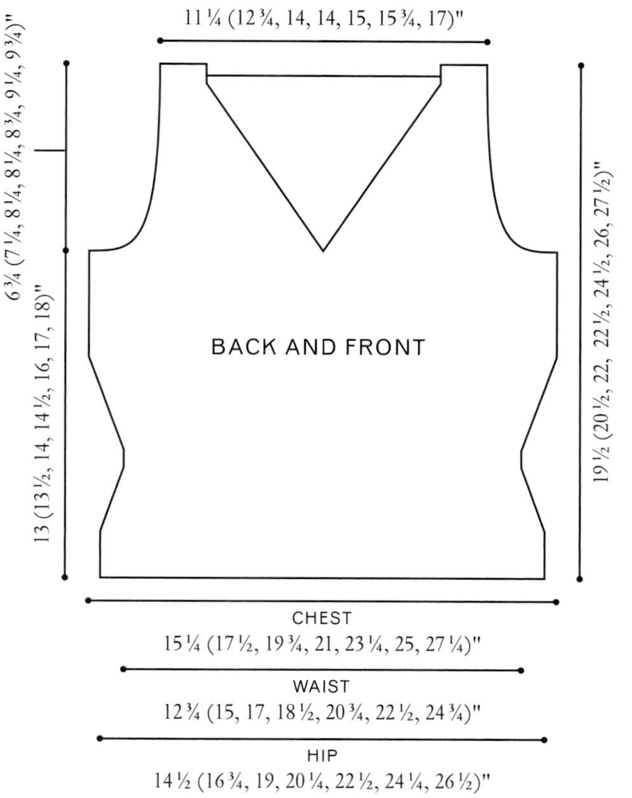
11¼ (12¾, 14, 14, 15, 15¾, 17)"
6¾ (7¼, 8¼, 8¼, 8¾, 9¼, 9¾)"
13 (13½, 14, 14½, 16, 17, 18)"
BACK AND FRONT
19½ (20½, 22, 22½, 24½, 26, 27½)"
CHEST
15¼ (17½, 19¾, 21, 23¼, 25, 27¼)"
WAIST
12¾ (15, 17, 18½, 20¾, 22½, 24¾)"
HIP
14½ (16¾, 19, 20¼, 22½, 24¼, 26½)"

3, 4) times AND AT SAME TIME, decrease 1 st at each neck edge every other row 17 (20, 22, 22, 23, 25, 26) times—8 (8, 9, 9, 10, 10, 12) sts remain at each shoulder.

Work even until shoulders measure same as Back from first underarm bind-off.

BO.

LEAVES (make 3)

Using crochet hook and A, ch 12, sc in 2nd chain from hook, hdc in next 2 chains, dc in next 3 chains, hdc in next chain, sc in next 3 chains, sc in last chain. Working on opposite side of starting chain, ch 1, sc in next 4 chains, hdc in next chain, dc in next 3 chains, hdc in next 2 chains, sc in next chain. Join and fasten off.

FLOWER #1

Rnd 1 : Using B, loosely ch 2, work 5 sc into 1st ch, join with sl st only in front loop of 1st sc.

Rnd 2: Working only in front loops of Rnd 1, [ch 4, sc in 2nd ch from hook, hdc in next ch, sc in next ch, sl st into next front loop] 5 times, join with sl st to first back loop of Rnd 1.

Rnd 3: Working only in back loops of Rnd 1, ch 1, 2 sc in same st, [2 sc in next st] 4 times, join with sl st in first front loop of this Rnd.

Rnd 4: Working only in front loops of Rnd 3, [ch 6, sc in 2nd ch from hook, hdc in next ch, (dc in next ch) 2 times, trc in next ch, skip 1 sc, sl st only to front loop of next sc] 5 times, ch 2, join with sl st in first back loop of Rnd 3.

Rnd 5: Working only in back loops of Rnd 3, ch 1, [sc, ch 3] 10 times, join with sl st to first sc of this Rnd.

Rnd 6: Sl st to ch 3 loop, ch 1, sc, [in next ch 3 loop work (2 dc, 2 trc, 1 dc, ch 3, sl st to 1st ch, 1 dc, 2 trc, 2 dc), in next ch 3 loop work sc] 5 times, ending with sl st join to 1st sc of this Rnd.

Fasten off.

FLOWER #2

Work as for Flower #1, using C for Rnds 1-2, D for rnds 3-4, and C for rnds 5-6.

FINISHING

Press Front and Back lightly.

Sew shoulder seams and side seams.

Carefully press completed leaves and flower petals with cool iron, taking care not to flatten.

Arrange flowers and leaves as shown in photo, and sew to shoulder of tank.

SURPLICE BODICE CAMISOLE

This camisole was inspired by the fashions of the French Revolution, when the empire waist was all the rage and a perky, high bosom was most desirable. Back then, women achieved this lifted look by lacing or wrapping a muslin sling under their breasts before they put their dresses on.

Here I've wrapped the bodice of this silk/linen camisole in a way that garners similarly fetching results—but is as beautiful as it is functional. The visible bust darts, surplice shaping, and ribbon lacing offer form as well as eye-catching detail, and a sheer lace stitch at the bottom adds a slimming, flirty touch.

FINISHED MEASUREMENTS
31 ½ (34, 38, 40 ½, 43 ½)" chest
20 (21, 22 ½, 23 ½, 25)" length from shoulder to hem
Camisole shown measures 31½" at chest

YARN
Classic Elite Interlude (70% linen / 30% silk; 82 yards / 50 grams): 6 (6, 7, 7, 8) skeins #20272 citron

NEEDLES
One pair straight needles size US 7 (4.5 mm)
One pair straight needles size US 6 (4 mm)
Change needle size if necessary to obtain correct gauge.

NOTIONS
Yarn needle
Stitch markers
1 ½ yards ¾" silk satin ribbon

GAUGE
18 sts and 24 rows = 4" (10 cm) in Stockinette stitch (St st) using larger needles

NOTES

This garment is knit in multiple directions: the bodices are knit from the bottom up, then stitches are picked up from the lower edge of the bodices and the lace bottom is knit from the top down.

STITCH PATTERN

Lace Pattern

(multiple of 6 sts + 1; 2-row repeat) (See Chart)

Row 1 (RS): K1, *yo, k1, k3tog, k1, yo, k1, repeat from *.

Row 2: P1, *k5, p1, repeat from *.

BACK

Using larger needles, CO 63 (69, 77, 83, 90) sts.

Working in St st, increase 1 st at each end of needle every 4 rows 4 times—71 (77, 85, 91, 98) sts.

Continuing in St st, work even until Back measures 3 ½ (4, 4 ½, 5, 5 ½)" from beginning.

Shape Armholes: BO 4 (4, 5, 6, 6) sts at beginning of next 2 rows and 3 (4, 4, 5, 5) sts at beginning of following 2 rows, then decrease 1 st at each end of needle every other row 2 (2, 3, 3, 3) times—53 (57, 61, 63, 70) sts.

Continuing in St st, work even until armholes measure 6 ½ (7, 7, 7 ½, 7 ½)".

Shape Shoulders: BO 5 (5, 5, 5, 6) sts at beginning of next 4 rows and 5 (5, 7, 7, 7) sts at beginning of following 2 rows.

BO remaining 23 (27, 27, 29, 32) sts for back neck.

RIGHT FRONT BODICE

Using larger needles, CO 46 (51, 55, 59, 63) sts.

Row 1 (RS): K26 (27, 25, 24, 24), pm, k to end.

Working in St st, yo before marker on every RS row 5 times to create bust dart and AT THE SAME TIME shape neck as follows: BO 2 sts at beginning of every RS row 10 times, then decrease 1 st at beginning of every RS row 4 times, then decrease 1 st at beginning of every other RS row 3 (7, 7, 9, 11) times. AT THE SAME TIME, continuing neck shaping, when bodice measures same as Back at side seam, shape armhole as follows: BO 4 (4, 5, 6, 6) sts at beginning of next WS row and 3 (4, 4, 5, 5) sts at beginning of following WS row, then decrease 1 st at armhole edge every other row 2 (2, 3, 3, 3) times.

Work even until bodice measures same as Back at armhole.

Shape shoulder as for Back.

LEFT FRONT BODICE

Using larger needles, CO 46 (51, 55, 59, 63) sts.

Row 1 (RS): K20 (24, 30, 35, 39), pm, k to end.

Working in St st, yo after marker on every RS row 5 times to create bust dart and AT THE SAME TIME shape neck as follows: BO 2 sts at beginning of every WS row 10 times, then decrease 1 st at beginning of every WS row 4 times, then decrease 1 st at beginning of every other WS row 3 (7, 7, 9, 11) times. AT THE SAME TIME, continuing neck shaping, when bodice measures same as Back at side seam, shape armhole as follows: BO 4 (4, 5, 6, 6) sts at beginning of next RS row and 3 (4, 4, 5, 5) sts at beginning of following RS row, then decrease 1 st at armhole edge every other row 2 (2, 3, 3, 3) times.

Work even until bodice measures same as Back at armhole.

Shape shoulder as for Back.

FINISHING

Sew shoulder seams.

Using smaller needles and with RS facing, pick up and knit 3 sts for every 4 rows and 1 st for every st along right front neck edge, back neck edge, and left front neck edge. Knit 2 rows and BO. Repeat along armhole edges.

Using smaller needles, pick up and knit 63 (69, 77, 83, 90) sts along cast-on edge of Back.

Row 1 (WS): Knit, increasing 4 (4, 2, 2, 1) st(s) evenly across row—67 (73, 79, 85, 91) sts.

Row 2: K1, *yo, k2tog, repeat from * to end.

Row 3: Knit.

Begin Lace Pattern and work even until lace measures 3" from beginning.

Change to larger needles and continue to work until lace measures 10 (10, 11, 11, 12)" from beginning. BO loosely.

Overlap fronts with each point just touching bottom of opposite bust dart. Sew fronts together at lower edge.

Using smaller needles, pick up and knit 67 (73, 79, 85, 91) sts along lower edge of fronts.

Row 1 (WS): Knit.

Row 2: K1, *yo, k2tog, repeat from * to end.

Row 3: Knit.

Work Lace Pattern as for Back. BO loosely.

Sew side seams. Steam garment lightly. Weave ribbon through eyelet holes and tie as shown.

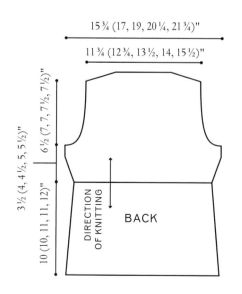

15 ¾ (17, 19, 20 ¼, 21 ¾)"

11 ¾ (12 ¾, 13 ½, 14, 15 ½)"

6 ½ (7, 7, 7 ½, 7 ½)"

3 ½ (4, 4 ½, 5, 5 ½)"

10 (10, 11, 11, 12)"

DIRECTION OF KNITTING

BACK

3 ¼ (3 ¼, 3 ¾, 3 ¾, 4 ¼)"

DIRECTION OF KNITTING

FRONT

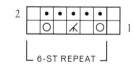

6-ST REPEAT

□ KNIT ON RS, PURL ON WS

• PURL ON RS, KNIT ON WS

○ YO

⟨ K3TOG

SILK AND PEARLS CAMI

This luxurious camisole would have been right at home in the Roaring Twenties, with its elegant pearl straps peeking out from under the shoulders of a sheer beaded frock. Silk lingerie was almost commonplace then, and the richer and more embellished, the better. The silhouette of this piece is simple—with a scoop neck, close shaping, and empire waist detail—but it doesn't lack for richness; the yarn is lustrous silk and the straps are made from strands of genuine freshwater pearls.

FINISHED MEASUREMENTS
30 (34, 38, 42, 46)" chest
12 ½ (13, 13 ½, 14, 14 ½)" length along side seam
Camisole shown measures 34" at chest

YARN
Classic Elite Temptation (100% silk; 110 yards /
   100 grams): 3 (4, 4, 5, 5) skeins #21 pearl blue

NEEDLES
One pair straight needles size US 9 (5.5 mm)
One pair straight needles size US 8 (5 mm)
Change needle size if necessary to obtain correct gauge.

NOTIONS
Stitch holder
Yarn needle
Sewing needle and matching thread
Two 16" strands of large freshwater pearls dyed to match
   yarn.

GAUGE
16 sts and 22 rows = 4" (10 cm) in Stockinette stitch
   (St st) using larger needles

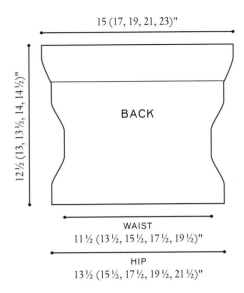

15 (17, 19, 21, 23)"

12 ½ (13, 13 ½, 14, 14 ½)"

BACK

WAIST
11 ½ (13 ½, 15 ½, 17 ½, 19 ½)"

HIP
13 ½ (15 ½, 17 ½, 19 ½, 21 ½)"

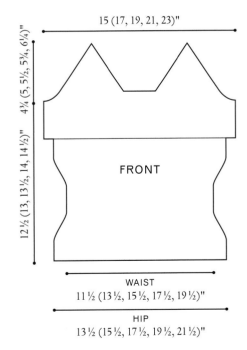

15 (17, 19, 21, 23)"

4 ¾ (5, 5 ½, 5 ¾, 6 ¼)"

12 ½ (13, 13 ½, 14, 14 ½)"

FRONT

WAIST
11 ½ (13 ½, 15 ½, 17 ½, 19 ½)"

HIP
13 ½ (15 ½, 17 ½, 19 ½, 21 ½)"

BACK

Using smaller needles, CO 54 (62, 70, 78, 86) sts.

Work in Garter st for 3 rows.

Change to larger needles and St st and work even until Back measures 1 ½ (1 ½, 2, 2, 2 ½)" from beginning.

Decrease 1 st at each end of needle every 4 rows 4 times— 46 (54, 62, 70, 78) sts.

Work 1 ½" even for waist area.

Increase 1 st at each end of needle every 4 rows 4 times— 54 (62, 70, 78, 86) sts.

Work even until Back measures 9 ½ (9 ½, 10, 10, 10 ½)" from beginning.

Work in Reverse St st for 2 rows.

Change to St st and increase 1 st at each end of needle every 4 rows 3 times—60 (68, 76, 84, 92) sts.

Work even until Back measures 12 ½ (13, 13 ½, 14, 14 ½)" from beginning.

Place sts on holder.

FRONT

Work as for Back until 2 rows of Reverse St st are completed.

Next RS row: Using M1 increases, increase 6 sts evenly across first row of bra—60 (68, 76, 84, 92) sts.

Work even until Front measures same as Back at side edges.

Shape Armholes: BO 3 (3, 4, 4, 4) sts at beginning of next 2 rows and 2 (2, 2, 3, 4) sts at the beginning of following 2 rows—50 (58, 64, 70, 76) sts remain.

Shape Neck:

Next RS row: K20 (24, 26, 28, 31) sts, BO 10 (10, 12, 14, 14) sts, knit to end—20 (24, 26, 28, 31) sts in each front.

Attach a second ball of yarn and work both fronts simultaneously, decreasing 1 st at each edge of each front every other row until 1 st remains in each front.

Fasten off.

FINISHING

Join Front to Back at right side seam.

Using smaller needles, pick up and knit sts for border along Front as follows: 1 st for each BO st, 3 sts for every 4 rows, and 1 extra st at point of each front. Knit across Back. Work 3 rows of Garter st. BO.

Sew remaining side seam.

Sew pearls onto front points securely. Pin at upper back and try on for fit. Sew at back.

Steam garment lightly.

chapter 5 THE STOCKING

Stockings have long served a functional purpose by covering the foot and leg for warmth, but only recently have they gained prestige as a fashion accessory. Their long, impressive history begins with the sock, the earliest known example of which dates back more than 3,000 years. It was during the fourth through tenth centuries, in Europe's colder climates, that socks evolved into long stockings, which were knitted in a tubular shape or sewn from bias-cut woven fabric, and tied or laced at the top. In England in 1589, the Reverend William Lee invented a machine that could produce stockings easily and quickly, but he was denied a patent by Queen Elizabeth in support of the hand-knitting industry. Still, Lee's machine became the forerunner of 19th-century sock-knitting machines that perfected the shaping of heels and toes, and machine-made stockings became widely available to women late that century.

Knit stockings remained the practical choice through the early 20th century. But after World War I, with the advent of shorter skirts, women traded in their modest wool stockings for long silk "nude" versions that allowed a glimpse of leg. These were held above the knee by garters, until skirts became even shorter and a belt worn around the waist onto which the stockings could clip was needed. Silk stockings gave way to nylon in the 1930s, which became the exclusive material for stockings after World War II. Until the late 1950s, these stockings were knitted flat and fully fashioned—shaped to fit the curves of the leg—and seamed up the back. In the 1960s, when skirts got still shorter, stockings became nearly extinct as pantyhose gained popularity.

Though gartered stockings are no longer worn on an everyday basis, today they are trotted out on special occasions when a bit of sex appeal is called for. All of the socks and stockings I've designed here are knit from the toe up, a technique that I like because I can try on and adjust the fit at any point in the process. I've also enjoyed working these pieces in an array of modern and luxury fibers. What could be more indulgent than an over-the-knee stocking in cashmere or a summer sock in an alpaca/silk blend? A soy-blend yarn gives a silky finish to my Fishnet Knee-Highs, and an elasticized cotton yarn makes my Tiny Tailored Gartini as practical as it is sexy.

BASIC STOCKINGS

The structure of a stocking consists of a toe, a foot, a heel, and a shaft (or leg). The shaft is not usually shaped in shorter socks, but to achieve a good fit for stockings or tall socks, some shaping is required. I've done this in the Basic Stocking with a series of increases that follow the contour of the leg.

I am quite partial to the peasant-style heel and toe, in which both are worked exactly the same in a modified short-row configuration. I like the smooth, tailored result. I've finished this stocking with ribbing at the top as well as eyelets with a ribbon tie, but for even more stay-up power (and this is true with any of the stockings in this chapter), elastic thread may be woven invisibly on the inside of the ribbing. Luxurious cashmere yarn, a lovely leaf-lace border, and rich velvet ribbon make these romantic stockings anything but basic.

SIZES
To fit ladies' shoe size 6 to 9

FINISHED MEASUREMENTS
17 ¼" long from top of heel

YARN
Knit One, Crochet Too Pure Cashmere (100% cashmere;
  88 yards / 25 grams): 7 balls #120 ivory

NEEDLES
One set of five double-pointed needles (dpn) size US 3
  (3.25 mm)
Change needle size if necessary to obtain correct gauge.

NOTIONS
Waste yarn
Stitch marker
1 ½ yards ½" velvet ribbon, brown
Elastic thread
Yarn needle

GAUGE
28 sts and 36 rnds = 4" (10 cm) in Stockinette stitch
  (St st)

KNIT ON RS, PURL ON WS

PURL ON RS, KNIT ON WS

SLIP AS IF TO PURL WITH YARN HELD TO WS

YO

K2TOG ON RS, P2TOG ON WS

P2TOG ON RS, K2TOG ON WS

BIND OFF 1 ST

NO STITCH

STITCH PATTERN

Oak-Leaf Edging Pattern
(from *A Treasury of Knitting Patterns* by Barbara G. Walker)
(panel of 10 sts, increased to 20 sts; 12-row repeat) (See Chart)

"A" portion of pattern: (Yo) twice, k2tog, (yo) twice, k2tog, k1.

"B" portion of pattern: Sl 1, (k2, p1) twice. (The purl sts are worked in the second loop of the double yo.)

Row 1 (WS): Sl 1, k2, yo, k2tog, A.

Row 2: B, k2, yo, k2tog, k1.

Row 3: Sl 1, k2, yo, k2tog, k2, A.

Row 4: B, k4, yo, k2tog, k1.

Row 5: Sl 1, k2, yo, k2tog, k4, A.

Row 6: B, k6, yo, k2tog, k1.

Row 7: Sl 1, k2, yo, k2tog, k6, A.

Row 8: B, k8, yo, k2tog, k1.

Row 9: Sl 1, k2, yo, k2tog, k8, A.

Row 10: B, k10, yo, k2tog, k1.

Row 11: Sl 1, k2, yo, k2tog, k15.

Row 12: BO 10, k to last 3 sts, yo, k2tog, k1.

Repeat Rows 1-12 for Oak-Leaf Edging Pattern.

TOE

Using provisional CO (see Special Techniques) and waste yarn, CO 26 sts.

Using main yarn and working back and forth on two needles, work first half of toe as follows:

Row 1 (WS): Purl.

Row 2: K1, ssk, k to last 3 sts, k2tog, k1.

Repeat Rows 1 and 2 until 8 sts remain in toe. Work second half of toe as follows:

Row 3: Purl.

Row 4: Pick up and knit 1 st from first half of toe, knit to end, pick up and knit 1 st from first half of toe.

Repeat Rows 3 and 4 until there are 26 sts on needles.

FOOT

Unravel provisional cast on, restoring 26 sts to needles—52 sts total on needles. Pm at one side of foot.

Distribute 13 sts to each of 4 dpns and work St st in the rnd until foot measures 4" from end of toe shaping or to desired length.

HEEL

Working heel back and forth on two needles and next 26 sts, repeat instructions for toe (omitting provisional cast on).

Place marker at center back of heel.

LEG

Begin working in the rnd on 4 needles again, and increase at each side of marker every 6 rnds 14 times—80 sts on needles.

Continuing in St st, work even for 46 rnds.

Work k2, p2 rib for 1".

Next rnd: *K2, yo, p2tog, repeat from * around.

Work k2, p2 rib for 1" more. BO.

LACE EDGING

CO 10 sts.

Work 10 repeats of Oak-Leaf Edging Pattern.

BO.

FINISHING

Seam lace edging into a circle. Slip over top of stocking and align top edge of lace just under row of eyelets on stocking. Stretch stocking top to fit lace and sew invisibly.

Thread yarn needle with elastic thread and work 4 rows of running stitch invisibly on inside of ribbing. Secure ends.

Weave velvet ribbon through eyelets and tie into bow. Cut to size.

Steam stockings and lace.

LACY SUMMER SOCKS

These openwork socks are short and comfortable, but delightfully feminine as well. The fiber is a luxurious blend of alpaca, silk, and cashmere, which creates a soft layer to hug delicate toes. The lace pattern is a simple two-row repeat worked from the bottom up, organically creating a pretty scalloped border at the top. I like to wear them with sandals or mules during warm weather—a pretty surprise under a flowing skirt or soft pants.

SIZES
To fit ladies' shoe size 6 to 9

FINISHED MEASUREMENTS
6 ¼" long from top of heel

YARN
Knit One, Crochet Too Ambrosia (70% baby alpaca / 20% silk / 10% cashmere; 137 yards / 50 grams): 2 balls #510 pale moss

NEEDLES
One set of five double-pointed needles size US 3 (3.25 mm)
Change needle size if necessary to obtain correct gauge.

NOTIONS
Waste yarn
Stitch marker

GAUGE
24 sts and 32 rnds = 4" (10 cm) in Stockinette stitch (St st)

STITCH PATTERN

Lace Pattern

(multiple of 13 sts; 2-rnd repeat) (See Chart)

Rnd 1: Knit.

Rnd 2: *K1, (k2tog) twice, (yo, k1) 3 times, yo, (ssk) twice, k1; repeat from *.

Repeat Rnds 1-2 for Lace Pattern.

13-ST REPEAT

	KNIT
O	YO
⋏	K2TOG
⋌	SSK

TOE

Using provisional cast on (see Special Techniques) and waste yarn, CO 26 sts.

Using main yarn and working back and forth on two needles, work first half of toe as follows:

Row 1 (WS): Purl.

Row 2: K1, ssk, k to last 3 sts, k2tog, k1.

Repeat Rows 1 and 2 until 8 sts remain in toe. Work second half of toe as follows:

Row 3: Purl.

Row 4: Pick up and knit 1 st from first half of toe, knit to end, pick up and knit 1 st from first half of toe.

Repeat Rows 3 and 4 until there are 26 sts on needles.

FOOT

Unravel provisional cast on, restoring 26 sts to needles—52 sts total on needles. Pm at one side of foot.

Distribute 13 sts to each of 4 needles and begin working in the rnd in Lace Pattern.

Work even until foot measures 4" from end of toe shaping or to desired length.

HEEL

Working heel back and forth on two needles and next 26 sts, repeat instructions for toe (omitting provisional cast on).

LEG

Begin working in the rnd on 4 needles again. Continue in Lace Pattern as established previously until leg measures 6" from top of heel.

Work 4 rows of Garter st. BO.

EMBROIDERED STOCKINGS

Makers of early machine-knitted hosiery faced a technical difficulty: The foot and the leg, usually made separately, required an obvious and unsightly seam when joined. Stocking-makers would cleverly disguise this seam by embroidering over and around it, thereby turning a "defect" into an attractive embellishment. During the 16th and 17th centuries, clock faces were the most popular motifs for this purpose, so much so that even when a different motif was used to hide the seam, such as flowers or fans, it was still called a clock.

These stockings feature a panel of traditional feather-and-fan stitch down the fronts and backs, and a pretty embroidered feather and fan at the ankle where clocks originally appeared. Not only is this stitch pretty, but it's an authentic motif. Fans were, after all, an accouterment of lady's attire once used for flirting with and attracting men. And feather quill pens were used to write secret love notes to the object of one's affection.

SIZES
Will stretch to fit all shoe sizes.

FINISHED MEASUREMENTS
Approximately 26 to 29" in length, stretched, measured
   from floor to top of stocking
Approximately 20" in length, unstretched, measured
   from end of heel to top of stocking

YARN
Cascade Yarns Fixation (98.3% cotton / 1.7% elastic;
   100 yards / 50 grams): 4 balls #2625 (MC)
Diakeito Diarufuran (100% wool; 161 yards / 40 grams):
   1 ball color #206 (A)
DMC Mouliné Special Effects embroidery floss (100%
   polyester / 8.7 yards / skein): 1 skein E3821 gold (B)

NEEDLES
One set of five double-pointed needles size US 3
   (3.25 mm)
One set of five double-pointed needles size US 6 (4 mm)
Change needle size if necessary to obtain correct gauge.

NOTIONS
Waste yarn
Stitch markers
Tailor's chalk
Yarn needle
Beading needle and sewing thread
Small amount of seed beads and pearls in matching
   colors

GAUGE
22 sts and 32 rnds = 4" (10 cm) in Stockinette stitch
   (St st) using smaller needles

STITCH PATTERN

Feather and Fan
(panel of 11 sts; 2-rnd repeat) (See Chart)

Rnd 1: (K2tog) twice, (yo, k1) 3 times, yo, (ssk) twice.

Rnd 2: Knit.

Repeat Rnds 1-2 for Feather and Fan.

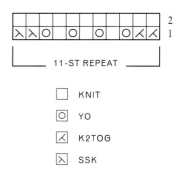

KNIT

YO

K2TOG

SSK

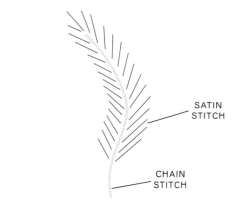

SATIN
STITCH

CHAIN
STITCH

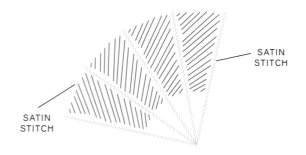

SATIN
STITCH

SATIN
STITCH

TOE

Using provisional cast on (see Special Techniques), waste yarn, and smaller needles, CO 25 sts.

Using MC and working back and forth on two needles, work first half of toe as follows:

Row 1 (WS): Purl.

Row 2: K1, ssk, k to last 3 sts, k2tog, k1.

Repeat Rows 1 and 2 until 7 sts remain in toe. Work second half of toe as follows:

Row 3: Purl.

Row 4: Pick up and knit 1 st from first half of toe, knit to end, pick up and knit 1 st from first half of toe.

Repeat Rows 3 and 4 until there are 25 sts on needles.

FOOT

Unravel provisional cast on, restoring 25 sts to needles—50 sts total on needles. Pm at one side of foot.

Distribute sts to 4 dpns and begin working in the rnd as follows: k7, pm, k11, pm, k to end of rnd.

Work Feather and Fan between markers and knit remaining sts until foot measures 4" from end of toe shaping or to desired length, ending with a plain knit rnd.

HEEL

Work across 25 instep sts; set aside. Working heel back and forth over remaining 25 sts, repeat instructions for toe (omitting provisional cast on). On last row of heel, k7, pm, k11, pm, k to end of heel.

LEG

Work Feather and Fan between markers on both front and back of leg, and knit remaining sts, until leg measures 4" from top of heel.

Change to larger needles.

Increase on each side of back lace panel every other rnd 9 times as follows: work to first marker on back of leg, M1, sm, work in pattern to second marker, sm, M1, work to end of rnd—68 sts on needles.

Work even for 2 ½".

Decrease on each side of back lace panel every 4 rnds 3 times as follows: work to within 2 sts of first marker on back of leg, ssk, sm, work in pattern to second marker, sm, k2tog, work to end of rnd—62 sts on needles.

Work even for 2 ½".

Increase as before on each side of back lace panel every 4 rnds 8 times—78 sts on needles.

Work even for 4" or desired length to top of stocking.

BO.

FINISHING

Using tailor's chalk, transfer motifs from diagram to stockings using photo as a guide for placement. Using yarn needle, embroider motifs in A and B. For best results, work embroidery with a tubular object approximately the circumference of your leg inserted into the stocking, stretching the stocking slightly. (Rolled newspaper of varying thickness can be very useful.)

Thread beading needle with sewing thread. Tie end of sewing thread around one bead. Load thread with 2" worth of beads. Sew firmly to bottom of fan. Repeat, sewing two beaded strands to each fan.

FISHNET KNEE-HIGHS

Fishnet stockings bring to mind images of cabaret girls, rock stars, pinups, and punks, all of whom have done their part to immortalize them. Once thought scandalous, in today's fashion climate they are a staple. My fishnets are worked in a worsted-weight yarn and a traditional diamond-shaped mesh pattern. I've handled the shaping in the shaft of this stocking a bit differently from the others in this chapter. By switching to a larger needle at the point of the calf rather than adding stitches, the circumference is enlarged without interfering with the mesh stitchwork.

SIZES
To fit ladies' shoe size 6 to 9

FINISHED MEASUREMENTS
16½" long from top of heel

YARN
Knit One, Crochet Too Wick (53% soy / 47%
   polypropylene; 120 yards / 50 grams): 3 balls color
   #533 avocado

NEEDLES
One set of five double-pointed needles size US 3
   (3.25 mm)
One set of five double-pointed needles size US 6
   (4 mm)
Change needle size if necessary to obtain correct gauge.

NOTIONS
Waste yarn

GAUGE
22 sts and 24 rnds = 4" (10 cm) in Stockinette stitch
   (St st) using smaller needles

STITCH PATTERN

Mesh Stitch
(multiple of 3 sts; 2-rnd repeat)

Rnd 1: *K1, yo, k2tog, repeat from * around.

Rnd 2: Knit.

TOE

Using provisional CO (see Special Techniques), smaller needles, and waste yarn, CO 24 sts.

Using main yarn and working back and forth on two needles, work first half of toe as follows:

Row 1 (WS): Purl.

Row 2: K1, ssk, k to last 3 sts, k2tog, k1.

Repeat Rows 1 and 2 until 8 sts remain in toe. Work second half of toe as follows:

Row 3: Purl.

Row 4: Pick up and knit 1 st from first half of toe, knit to end, pick up and knit 1 st from first half of toe.

Repeat Rows 3 and 4 until there are 24 sts on needles.

FOOT

Unravel provisional cast on, restoring 24 sts to needles—48 sts total on needles. Pm at one side of foot.

Distribute 12 sts to each of 4 dpns and join for working in the round.

Next round: *K2, k2tog, repeat from * around—36 sts on needles.

Next round: Knit.

Work in Mesh st until foot measures 4 ½" or desired length from end of toe shaping, ending with a knit round.

HEEL

Work across 18 instep sts; set aside. Work across remaining 18 sts for heel as follows: [K2, M1, k1] 6 times—24 sts in heel.

Working back and forth on two needles and 24 heel sts, repeat instructions for toe (omitting provisional cast on).

Next RS row: [K2, k2tog] 6 times—18 sts in heel.

LEG

Begin working in the rnd on 4 needles again. Continuing in Mesh st, work even until sock measures 4 ½" from top of heel.

Change to larger needles and work even for 10".

Next rnd: *K2, M1, k1, repeat from * around—48 sts on needles.

Change to smaller needles and work in k2, p2 rib for 2".

BO loosely in rib.

TINY TAILORED GARTINI

I'm sure that the main reason stockings fell out of favor in the 1960s was the garter belt or girdle needed to hold them up. These gadgets, in addition to panties, slips, and stockings, made for a lot of bulk and fuss under clothing. Once women discovered the convenience and comfort of panty hose, stockings didn't stand a chance. There are, however, times when stockings may still be a desirable option, such as during warm weather or just when you want to feel a little sexier. For those times, I offer the simple and functional Gartini, which is a panty onto which adjustable garter straps are attached.

SIZES
To fit 25 (30, 34)" high hip

FINISHED MEASUREMENTS
23 (27, 31)" high hip
Gartini shown measures 23"

YARN
Cascade Yarns Fixation (98.3% cotton / 1.7% elastic;
  100 yards / 50 grams): 1 (1, 2) balls color #2625 (MC)
Diakeito Diarufuran (100% wool; 161 yards / 40 grams):
  1 ball color #206 (CC)

NEEDLES
One pair straight needles size US 7 (4.5 mm)
Change needle size if necessary to obtain correct gauge.

NOTIONS
Yarn needle
1½ yards 1" elastic
Sewing needle and thread, for securing elastic
4 ½" slides
4 ½" garter grips
Decorative 10 mm bead

GAUGE
20 sts and 28 rows = 4" (10 cm) in Stockinette stitch
  (St st) using MC, unstretched

PANTY

Using MC, CO 25 (30, 35) sts.

Work even in St st for 2 rows.

Decrease 1 st at each end of needle every 4 rows 9 (10, 11) times—7 (10, 13) sts.

Work even for 10 rows.

Increase 1 st at each end of needle every other row 10 times, then every 4 rows 6 (7, 8) times—39 (44, 49) sts.

Work even for 20 rows. BO.

LEG BANDS

Using MC and with RS facing, pick up and knit 3 sts for every 4 rows along left leg opening.

Working in Garter st, knit 1 row.

Change to CC and knit 2 rows.

Change to MC and knit 1 row. BO.

Repeat for right leg band.

WAISTBAND

Using MC and with RS facing, pick up and knit 39 (44, 49) sts across back of panty, CO 25 (30, 35) sts, pick up and knit 25 (30, 35) sts across front of panty, CO 25 (30, 35) sts—114 (134, 154) sts.

Knit 1 row.

Change to CC and knit 2 rows.

Change to MC and work in St st for 4 rows.

Change to CC and knit 2 rows.

Change to MC and knit 1 row. BO.

SUSPENDERS (make 4)

Using MC, CO 4 sts.

Work in Garter st until suspender measures 9" stretched. BO.

FINISHING

Sew ends of waistband together at right back.

Using yarn needle and yarn, embroider a row of V's (see Special Techniques—Casing for Elastic) on inside of waistband to make casing for elastic, making sure embroidery is invisible on outside. Cut elastic to desired length, and thread through casing. Using sewing needle and thread, secure ends of elastic.

Place slide on suspender strap, thread strap through garter grip, and secure end of strap under slide (see Special Techniques—Suspender Assembly). Sew suspenders to bottom of waistband, 1½" away from front and back of panty as shown in photo.

Sew decorative bead to front waistband.

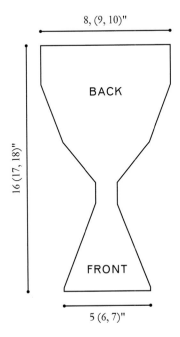

LOUNGE / NIGHT WEAR

chapter 6

Throughout this book, I've focused on specific categories of lingerie—the bra, the stocking, the corset, and so on. However, countless other forms of lingerie exist that defy categorization, each with its own purpose and history. Loosely collected under the categories of loungewear and nightwear, all of the pieces featured here were originally designed to be kept under cover—as an undergarment or an item meant only to be worn around the house. But like the rest of the lingerie in this book, each piece has since made the leap to modern outerwear—or, in some cases, provocative, playful nightwear. Each, also, is uniquely suited for knitting and, traditionally, was a knitted item.

The Racerback Tank and Leggings with Mesh Sides have come a long way from antique swimwear and a man's union suit, respectively, to become the comfortable, versatile layering pieces they are here. The Basic Baby Doll is a piece of nightwear that, layered over a tank top, could work just as well in public as in private. The Bed Jacket, once designed to cover a bed-ridden woman modestly when visitors were received, is now a romantic cardigan that begs to be worn out. The Arm Warmers remind us that though our ancestors had to deal with less comfortable conditions than we do today, they were innovative and clever and enjoyed a great sense of style.

BASIC BABY DOLL AND PANTY

A baby doll is a small nightgown or negligee for women, often trimmed with lace and usually short enough to expose its matching panty. The style originated in the 1930s for little girls, hence the name "baby doll." However, it was transformed into a provocative garment for women when starlet Caroll Baker wore one in the notorious 1956 movie Baby Doll, *based on a Tennessee Williams screenplay.*

This lacy baby doll, luxurious but a little notorious as well, is knit in a pure silk yarn and comes complete with a matching thong panty.

FINISHED MEASUREMENTS
Baby doll: 33 (36, 38, 41, 44, 48, 52, 55)" chest
Thong panty: 35 (37, 39, 41, 44, 48, 50, 52)" high hip
   (4"-5" below natural waist) prior to elastic insertion
Baby doll shown measures 33"; thong panty shown
   measures 35"

YARN
Adrienne Vittadini Celia (100% silk; 109 yards /
   25 grams): 5 (6, 6, 7, 7, 8, 8, 9) balls #4543 dusty teal

NEEDLES
One 24" circular needle size US 6 (4 mm)
One 24" circular needle size US 8 (5 mm)
One circular needle size US 10 (6 mm)
Change needle size if necessary to obtain correct gauge.

NOTIONS
Yarn needle
2 (2, 2 ¼, 2 ½, 2 ½, 2 ¾, 3, 3) yards ¼" lingerie elastic
Sewing needle and matching thread

GAUGE
20 sts and 28 rows = 4" (10 cm) in Stockinette st (St st)
   using size US 6 (4 mm) needles

NOTES

The baby doll is knit in multiple directions: the back and front bodices are knit from the bottom up, then stitches are picked up from the lower edge of the bodices and the lace bottom is knit from the top down.

The baby doll and thong panty are worked flat, yet circular needles are required to knit the baby doll's lace bottom.

STITCH PATTERN

Lace Pattern

(multiple of 12 sts + 1; 2-row repeat) (See Chart)

Row 1 (RS): K1, *(k2tog) twice, (yo, k1) 3 times, yo, (ssk) twice, k1, repeat from *.

Row 2: Purl.

Repeat Rows 1-2 for Lace Pattern.

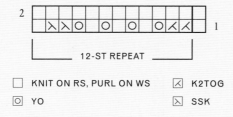

KNIT ON RS, PURL ON WS ☐   K2TOG ⟋

YO ◯   SSK ⟍

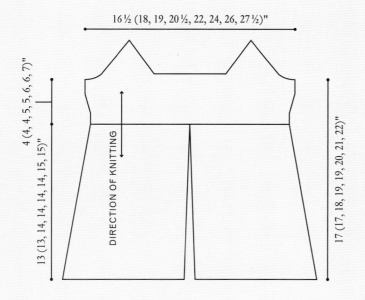

BABY DOLL

BACK

Using size US 6 (4 mm) needles, CO 79 (86, 91, 99, 106, 116, 126, 133) sts. Do not join.

Work in St st for 1".

Increase 1 st at each end of needle every 6 rows 2 times—83 (90, 95, 103, 110, 120, 130, 137) sts.

Work even until Back measures 4 (4, 4, 5, 5, 6, 6, 7)" from beginning.

Shape Armhole and Neck: BO 5 (5, 5, 7, 7, 8, 9, 11) sts at the beginning of next 2 rows and 3 (3, 4, 5, 5, 7, 8, 10) sts at beginning of following 2 rows—67 (74, 77, 79, 86, 90, 96, 95) sts.

Next RS row: K21 (21, 23, 23, 25, 25, 27, 27), BO 25 (32, 31, 33, 36, 40, 42, 41), k to end.

Attach a second ball of yarn and work both shoulders simultaneously, decreasing 1 st at each edge of each shoulder until 1 st remains. Fasten off.

FRONT

Work as for Back until Front measures 2 ½ (2 ½, 2 ½, 3 ½, 3 ½, 4, 4 ½, 4 ½)"; end ready to work a RS row.

Shape Bust: For cup sizes C and larger, shape bust with short rows as follows:

Row 1 (RS): Work to within 3 sts of of end of row, wrp-t (see Special Techniques—Short Row Shaping).

Row 2: Work to within 3 sts of end of row, wrp-t.

Rows 3 and 4: Work to within 4 sts of end of row, wrp-t.

Rows 5 and 6: Work to within 5 sts of end of row, wrp-t.

Continue working additional short rows, each 1 st shorter than than the previous, until an appropriate number of sts have been wrapped on each side of front: 6 sts for a C cup, 12 sts for a D cup, 18 sts for a DD cup, and so on.

Next 2 rows: Work to end of row, working wraps with the sts they wrap.

Continuing in St st, work even until Front measures same as Back at side seams.

Shape armhole and neck as for Back.

LOWER BODY

Steam Front and Back lightly, and sew side seams.

Using size US 6 (4 mm) needle and beginning at center front, pick up and knit 145 (145, 169, 169, 181, 181, 217, 217) sts along lower edge of bodice.

Leaving center front open and working back and forth on circular needle, work in Lace Pattern until lower body measures 2" from bottom of bodice.

Change to size US 8 (5 mm) needle and continue for 2" more.

Change to size US 10 (6 mm) needle and continue until garment measures 17 (17, 18, 19, 19, 20, 21, 22)" from underarm to hem. BO very loosely.

FINISHING

Using size US 6 (4 mm) needle, pick up and knit 3 sts for every 4 rows and 1 st for every st along Back neckline. Work 3 rows in Garter st, then BO. Repeat for Front.

CO 50 (50, 55, 55, 60, 60, 65, 65) sts, beg at back left underarm, pick up and knit 3 sts for every 4 rows and 1 st for every 1 st from back to front along left underarm, then CO 50 (50, 55, 55, 60, 60, 65, 65) sts. Work 3 rows in Garter st, then BO. Repeat at right underarm, working from front to back. Tie straps at shoulders.

Using yarn needle and yarn, embroider a row of V's (see Special Techniques—Casing for Elastic) on inside of bottom of bodice to make casing for elastic, making sure embroidery is invisible on outside. Cut elastic to desired length, and thread through casing. Using sewing needle and thread, secure ends of elastic.

Steam bodice and straps lightly.

Wet lace and steam, letting lace open up and grow in length, making sure length is even all around baby doll.

THONG PANTY

FRONT

Using size US 6 (4 mm) needles, CO 35 sts.

Working in St st, decrease 1 st at each end of needle every 4 rows until 1 st remains. Fasten off.

BACK STRAP

Pick up and knit 3 sts for every 4 rows from top to bottom along right edge of Front, then CO 40 (40, 44, 44, 48, 48, 52, 52) sts for back strap of thong. Work 3 rows in Garter st, then BO.

Pick up and knit 40 (40, 44, 44, 48, 48, 52, 52) sts along back strap, then 3 sts for every 4 rows along left edge of Front. Work 3 rows in Garter st, then BO.

WAISTBAND

CO 140 (150, 160, 170, 185, 205, 215, 225) sts, then pick up and knit 35 sts across top front of thong.

Work 3 rows in Garter st.

Next row: K1 (1, 1, 1, 2, 2, 2, 2), *yo, k2tog, repeat from *.

Work 3 rows in Garter st, then BO.

FINISHING

Sew waistband together at top right corner of front of thong. Sew back strap of thong to center back of waistband.

Cut elastic to desired length, and thread through eyelets of waistband. Using sewing needle and thread, secure ends of elastic.

Steam thong lightly.

BED JACKET

During the 18th century, both women and men wore their chemises to bed as a sort of nightgown—the era of removing undergarments at the end of the day or for washing had not yet arrived. The bed jacket became a popular garment for women because it could be worn over the chemise if receiving visitors while in bed (not an uncommon practice at the time). It could also be worn around the house over a corset and petticoat, like a modern housecoat, and while engaging in such ladylike tasks as writing letters or doing needlework. Early 20th-century bed jackets, also known as "boudoir" or "combing" jackets, were commonly knitted—sometimes with lots of fancy lace details—and looked very much like shawls with a knitted cuff at either end. They became a common gift for a new mother to wear while she was still in the hospital, and were sometimes paired with a matching jacket for baby.

The body of this bed jacket is worked in Stockinette stitch with set-in sleeves for a smooth, tailored fit. The flounces are knit in a Garter stitch and eyelet combination with short rows to fit around the curves of the jacket smoothly and to give the edges some flare.

FINISHED MEASUREMENTS
30 (34 ½, 39, 43 ½, 48, 52 ½, 57)" chest
20 ½ (21, 22 ½, 23, 23 ½, 24 , 24 ½)" length
12 (12, 13 ½, 13 ½, 14, 15, 15 ½)" sleeve length to
  underarm
Jacket shown measures 34 ½" at chest

YARN
Cascade Sierra (80% cotton / 20% wool; 191 yards /
  100 grams): 6 (6, 7, 7, 8, 8, 9) skeins #51

NEEDLES
One pair straight needles size US 9 (5.5 mm)
Change needle size if necessary to obtain correct gauge.

NOTIONS
Crochet hook size US G/6 (4 mm)
Yarn needle
One 1" decorative button
One large snap set
Sewing needle and thread, for securing snap set

GAUGE
18 sts and 24 rows = 4" (10 cm) in Stockinette stitch
  (St st)

STITCH PATTERNS

Edging Pattern 1

(multiple of 4 sts + 1; 10-row repeat)

Row 1 (WS): Knit.

Rows 2-9: Knit.

Row 10: *P2, yo, p2tog, repeat from * to last st, end p1.

Repeat Rows 1-10 for Edging Pattern 1.

Edging Pattern 2

(multiple of 4 sts + 1; 10-row repeat)

Row 1 (WS): Knit.

Row 2: Knit.

Row 3: K20 (20, 24, 24, 24, 29, 29), wrp-t (see Special Techniques—Short Row Shaping).

Row 4: Knit.

Row 5: K18 (18, 22, 22, 22, 27, 27), wrp-t.

Rows 6, 7, 8, and 9: Knit.

Row 10: *P2, yo, p2tog, repeat from * to last st, end p1.

Repeat Rows 1-10 for Edging Pattern 2.

BACK

CO 58 (68, 78, 88, 98, 108, 118) sts.

Work in St st for 1".

Increase 1 st at each end of needle every 6 rows 5 times—68 (78, 88, 98, 108, 118, 128) sts.

Continuing in St st, work even until Back measures 8 (8 ½, 8 ½, 9, 9, 10, 10)" from beginning.

Shape Armholes: BO 3 (4, 5, 6, 8, 8, 9) sts at beginning of next 2 rows, and 2 (3, 4, 4, 5, 7, 8) sts at beginning of following 2 rows.

Decrease 1 st at each end of needle every other row 1 (2, 3, 3, 3, 3, 4) times—56 (60, 64, 72, 76, 82, 86) sts remain.

Continuing in St st, work even until armholes measure 6 ½ (6 ½, 7, 7, 7 ½, 8, 8 ½)".

Shape Shoulders and Neck: With RS facing, BO 4 (4, 5, 6, 6, 6, 6) sts at beginning of next 2 rows, 4 (4, 5, 6, 6, 6, 6) sts at beginning of following 2 rows, and 4 (4, 5, 5, 5, 7, 7) sts at beginning of following 2 rows.

BO remaining 32 (36, 34, 38, 42, 44, 48) sts for neck.

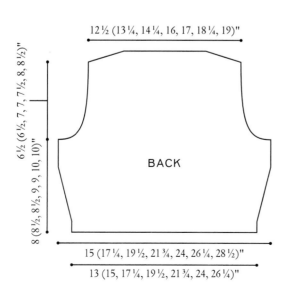

12 ½ (13 ¼, 14 ¼, 16, 17, 18 ¼, 19)"

6 ½ (6 ½, 7, 7, 7 ½, 8, 8 ½)"

8 (8 ½, 8 ½, 9, 9, 10, 10)"

BACK

15 (17 ¼, 19 ½, 21 ¾, 24, 26 ¼, 28 ½)"

13 (15, 17 ¼, 19 ½, 21 ¾, 24, 26 ¼)"

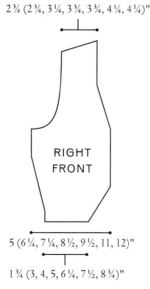

2 ¾ (2 ¾, 3 ¼, 3 ¾, 3 ¾, 4 ¼, 4 ¼)"

RIGHT FRONT

5 (6 ¼, 7 ¼, 8 ½, 9 ½, 11, 12)"

1 ¾ (3, 4, 5, 6 ¼, 7 ½, 8 ¾)"

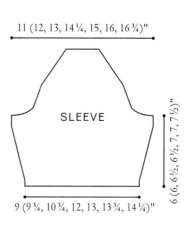

11 (12, 13, 14 ¼, 15, 16, 16 ¾)"

SLEEVE

6 (6, 6 ½, 6 ½, 7, 7, 7 ½)"

9 (9 ¾, 10 ¾, 12, 13, 13 ¾, 14 ¼)"

LEFT FRONT

CO 8 (13, 18, 23, 28, 34, 39) sts.

Working in St st, increase 1 st at center front edge every other row 10 times and AT THE SAME TIME, when side seam edge measures 1" from beginning, increase 1 st at side seam edge every 6 rows 5 times—23 (28, 33, 38, 43, 49, 54) sts.

Continuing in St st, work even until Left Front measures same as Back at side seam.

Shape Armhole and V-Neck: Shape armhole as for Back and AT THE SAME TIME decrease 1 st at neck edge every 4 rows 5 (7, 6, 8, 10, 10, 9) times, then every other row 0 (0, 0, 0, 0, 2, 5) times.

Continuing in St st, work even until armhole measures same as for Back.

Shape Shoulder: BO remaining 12 (12, 15, 17, 17, 19, 19) sts at shoulder same as for Back.

RIGHT FRONT

Work same as for Left Front, reversing all shaping.

SLEEVES (make 2)

CO 40 (44, 48, 54, 58, 62, 66) sts.

Work in St st for ½".

Increase 1 st at each end of needle every 6 rows 5 times— 50 (54, 58, 64, 68, 72, 76) sts on needles.

Continuing in St st, work even until sleeve measures 6 (6, 6 ½, 6 ½, 7, 7, 7 ½)" from beginning.

Shape Cap: BO 3 (4, 5, 6, 8, 8, 9) sts at beginning of next 2 rows, and 2 (3, 4, 4, 5, 7, 8) sts at beginning of following 2 rows.

Decrease 1 st at each end of needle every 4 rows 0 (2, 3, 2, 3, 5, 6) times, then every other row 14 (11, 10, 12, 10, 7, 6) times. BO remaining 12 (14, 14, 16, 16, 18, 18) sts.

UPPER COLLAR EDGING

CO 25 (25, 29, 29, 29, 33, 33) sts.

Work in Edging Pattern 1 until edging reaches from point A of front to point B (see Bodice Diagram on page 142); end having worked Row 10.

Change to Edging Pattern 2 and work until short selvedge of edging reaches from point B to point C; end having worked Row 10.

Change back to Edging Pattern 1 and work until edging reaches from point C to point D. BO.

LOWER EDGING

CO 25 (25, 29, 29, 29, 33, 33) sts.

Work in Edging Pattern 2 until short selvedge of edging reaches from point A to point D around bottom of body (see Bodice Diagram below).

BO.

SLEEVE EDGINGS (make 2)

CO 25 (25, 29, 29, 29, 33, 33) sts.

Work in Edging Pattern 2 until short selvedge of edging is same length as bottom of sleeve.

BO.

BODICE DIAGRAM

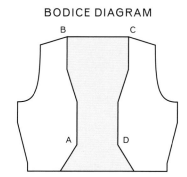

EDGING DIAGRAM

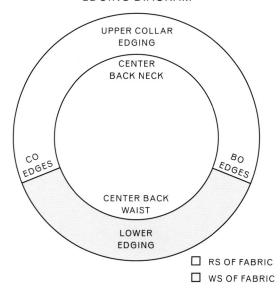

☐ RS OF FABRIC
☐ WS OF FABRIC

FINISHING

Lightly steam all pieces.

Sew side seams and shoulder seams.

Sew WS of CO edge of Upper Collar Edging to RS of CO edge of Lower Edging (see Edging Diagram below left).

Sew WS of BO edge of Upper Collar Edging to RS of BO edge of Lower Edging.

Sew short selvedge of body edging to body of jacket, easing at lower front edges.

Sew short selvedge of sleeve edgings to bottom of sleeves.

With crochet hook, work picot edge around outer edge of jacket as follows: attach yarn, *[ch 3, skip 2 Garter ridges or 2 St st rows, sc in next row] twice, ch 5, sc in same row as previous sc, repeat from *. Repeat for each sleeve.

Thread yarn needle with yarn. Embroider a chain stitch on outside of jacket where edging meets body. Repeat for each sleeve.

Sew sleeve seam. Set sleeve into armhole.

Press garment lightly.

Try garment on. Determine placement of button along chain stitch embroidery on RS of Left Front. Sew button in place. Sew one half of snap set to matching point on WS of Right Front, and other half of snap set to edge of Left Front. Pass button through crochet loop or yo eyelet.

LEGGINGS WITH MESH SIDES

The origins of these mesh-sided leggings are hardly romantic—they are inspired by the union suit, a type of one-piece long underwear favored by men who work outside and for hunting, but also worn by women in cold climates. Originally, in the 1800s, these garments were made of woven flannel, but were later fashioned of knit jersey. Eventually the union suit was split up into separate tops and bottoms, and became known as long johns. Such close-fitting underwear may also have inspired later outerwear fashions, such as the slim cigarette pants favored by women in the 1950s, the stirrup pants of the early 1960s, and the leggings of the 1980s.

For these mesh-sided leggings, I chose an elasticized cotton yarn that assures a great fit (with no worries about baggy knees) and is cool enough to be comfortable, yet warm enough to be cozy. The mesh stitch on the sides is a simple yarnover pattern, but it adds interest and lets a little flesh show through tastefully.

SIZES
To fit 29 ½-31 (32-34, 35-36 ½, 37 ½-39, 40-41, 43-44)" full hip

FINISHED MEASUREMENTS
28 ½ (31, 33, 36 ½, 39, 41)" high hip (4"-5" below natural waist)
29 (31½, 34, 37, 39 ½, 42)" full hip (widest area around buttocks)
26 (26 ½, 27, 27 ½, 28, 28 ¾)" inseam
Leggings shown measure 31" at high hip

YARN
Cascade Fixation (98.3% cotton / 1.7% elastic; 100 yards / 50 grams): 7 (7, 8, 9, 10, 11) balls #7988 chocolate

NEEDLES
One pair straight needles size US 7 (4.5 mm)
Change needle size if necessary to obtain correct gauge.

NOTIONS
Stitch markers
Yarn needle
1½ yards ½" elastic
Sewing needle and thread

GAUGE
20 sts and 28 rows = 4" (10 cm) in Stockinette stitch (St st)

STITCH PATTERN

Mesh Pattern

(multiple of 5 sts; 2-row repeat)

Row 1 (RS): *K2tog, yo, k1, yo, ssk, repeat from *.

Row 2: Purl.

Repeat these two rows for Mesh Pattern.

LEFT LEG

CO 45 (47, 49, 51, 55, 59) sts.

Row 1 (RS): Knit.

Row 2: Knit.

Row 3: K15 (16, 17, 18, 20, 22), pm, k15, pm, k15 (16, 17, 18, 20, 22).

Row 4: Knit.

Next row, work 15 (16, 17, 18, 20, 22) sts in St st, work Mesh Pattern between markers, work 15 (16, 17, 18, 20, 22) sts in St st.

Shape Inseam: Increase 1 st at each end of needle every 6 rows 22 (23, 23, 25, 25, 25) times, then every 4 rows 3 (4, 4, 5, 6, 7) times—95 (101, 103, 111, 117, 123) sts.

Increase 1 st only at beginning of needle every 4 rows an additional 4 times—99 (105, 107, 115, 121, 127) sts.

Continuing in St st and Mesh Pattern as established, work even until leg measures 26 (26 ½, 27, 27 ½, 28, 28 ¾)" from beginning; end ready to work a RS row.

Shape Crotch: BO 6 sts at beginning of next RS row and 4 sts at beginning of following WS row—89 (95, 97, 105, 111, 117) sts.

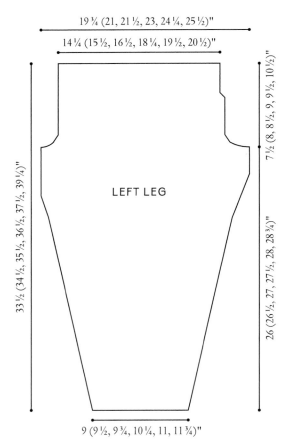

19 ¾ (21, 21 ½, 23, 24 ¼, 25 ½)"

14 ¼ (15 ½, 16 ½, 18 ¼, 19 ½, 20 ½)"

7 ½ (8, 8 ½, 9, 9 ½, 10 ½)"

LEFT LEG

33 ½ (34 ½, 35 ½, 36 ½, 37 ½, 39 ¼)"

26 (26 ½, 27, 27 ½, 28, 28 ¾)"

9 (9 ½, 9 ¾, 10 ¼, 11, 11 ¾)"

BO 5 (5, 4, 4, 4, 4) sts at beginning of next RS row and 3 (3, 2, 2, 2, 2) sts at beginning of following WS row—81 (87, 91, 99, 105, 111) sts.

Decrease 1 st at each end of needle every other row 4 (4, 3, 3, 3, 3) times—73 (79, 85, 93, 99, 105) sts.

Work even until leg measures 5" from first set of bind-offs.

Decrease 1 st only at beginning of needle on next 2 RS rows— 71 (77, 83, 91, 97, 103) sts.

Work even until leg measures 7 (7 ½, 8, 8 ½, 9, 10)" from first set of bind-offs.

Work in Garter st for 6 rows.

BO.

RIGHT LEG

Work as for Left Leg, reversing all shaping.

FINISHING

Using yarn needle and yarn, fold Left Leg in half lengthwise and sew left inseam. Repeat for Right Leg. Sew center seam to join Left Leg to Right Leg.

Using yarn needle and yarn, embroider a row of V's (see Special Techniques—Casing for Elastic) on inside of waistband to make casing for elastic, making sure embroidery is invisible on outside. Cut elastic to desired length, and thread through casing. Using sewing needle and thread, secure ends of elastic.

Press garment lightly.

RACERBACK TANK WITH MESH SIDES

This top evolved out of the body-hugging wool jersey sleeveless bathing suits of the 1920s, which were ideal for the athletic, androgynous figure that modern fashions suited best. The fabrication, however, left a lot to be desired, as the wool stretched when wet, and if not knitted firmly enough, the suits compromised a lady's modesty in other ways.

This racerback tank was inspired by the tops of these suits, and it hints at the modern sports bra. The elasticized cotton yarn alleviates any worry about stretching, and the mesh sides expose just the right amount of skin to be modest, yet intriguing.

SIZES
To fit 29 ½-32 (32 ½-35, 35 ½-39, 39 ½-42, 42 ½-46, 46 ½- 49)" chest

FINISHED MEASUREMENTS
29 (32, 35, 39 ¼, 43, 47 ¼)" chest
26 ½ (29 ½, 33, 36 ¾, 41, 44 ¾)" waist
Tank shown measures 32" at chest

YARN
Cascade Fixation (98.3% cotton / 1.7% elastic; 100 yards / 50 grams): 3 (4, 5, 6, 7, 8) balls #7988 chocolate

NEEDLES
One pair straight needles size US 7 (4.5 mm)
One pair straight needles size US 6 (4 mm)
Change needle size if necessary to obtain correct gauge.

NOTIONS
Stitch markers
Yarn needle

GAUGE
20 sts and 28 rows = 4" (10 cm) in Stockinette stitch (St st) using larger needles

STITCH PATTERN

Mesh Pattern

(multiple of 5 sts; 2-row repeat)

Row 1 (RS): *K2tog, yo, k1, yo, ssk, repeat from *.

Row 2: Purl.

Repeat these two rows for Mesh Pattern.

FRONT

Using smaller needles, CO 81 (89, 97, 105, 117, 125) sts.

Row 1 (RS): Knit.

Row 2: Knit.

Row 3: K15, pm, k51 (59, 67, 75, 87, 95), pm, k15.

Row 4: Knit.

Next row, change to larger needles and work Mesh Pattern to first marker, work St st between markers, and work Mesh Pattern after second marker.

Continuing in Mesh Pattern and St st as established, work even for 2".

Increase 1 st at beginning and end of St st panel every 10 rows 3 times—87 (95, 103, 111, 123, 131) sts.

Work even until Front measures 11 (12, 13, 14, 15, 16)" from beginning.

Shape Armholes: BO 15 sts at beginning of next 2 rows, then 2 (3, 3, 3, 6, 7) sts at beginning of following 2 rows—53 (59, 67, 75, 81, 87) sts.

Decrease 1 st at each end of needle every other row 1 (1, 1, 1, 3, 3) time(s)—51 (57, 65, 73, 75, 81) sts.

Work even until armholes measure 1½" from first underarm BO; end ready to work a RS row.

Shape Neck: Work across 15 (17, 17, 19, 21, 23) sts, BO 21 (23, 31, 35, 33, 35) sts, work remaining sts—15 (17, 17, 19, 21, 23) sts in each shoulder.

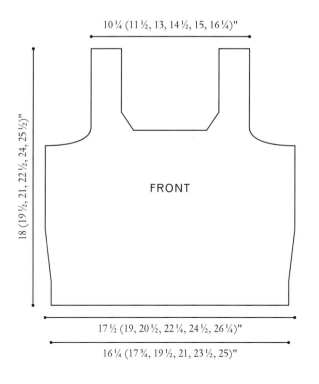

10 ¼ (11 ½, 13, 14 ½, 15, 16 ¼)"

18 (19 ½, 21, 22 ½, 24, 25 ½)"

FRONT

17 ½ (19, 20 ½, 22 ¼, 24 ½, 26 ¼)"

16 ¼ (17 ¾, 19 ½, 21, 23 ½, 25)"

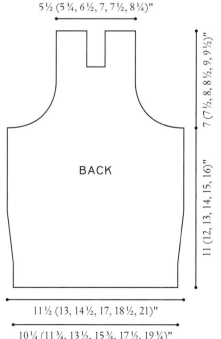

5 ½ (5 ¾, 6 ½, 7, 7 ½, 8 ¼)"

7 (7 ½, 8, 8 ½, 9, 9 ½)"

11 (12, 13, 14, 15, 16)"

BACK

11 ½ (13, 14 ½, 17, 18 ½, 21)"

10 ¼ (11 ¾, 13 ½, 15 ¾, 17 ½, 19 ¾)"

Attach second ball of yarn. Working both shoulders simultaneously, decrease 1 st at each neck edge every other row 5 times—10 (12, 12, 14, 16, 18) sts in each shoulder.

Work even until shoulders measure 7 (7 ½, 8, 8 ½, 9, 9 ½)" from first underarm BO.

BO.

BACK

Using smaller needles, CO 51 (59, 67, 79, 87, 99) sts.

Work in Garter st for 4 rows.

Change to larger needles and work St st for 2".

Increase 1 st at each end of needle every 10 rows 3 times— 57 (65, 73, 85, 93, 105) sts.

Work even until Back measures 11 (12, 13, 14, 15, 16)" from beginning.

Shape Armholes: BO 4 (5, 5, 7, 8, 9) sts at beginning of the next 6 rows, then decrease 1 st at each end of needle every 4 rows 3 (3, 5, 4, 4, 5) times—27 (29, 33, 35, 37, 41) sts.

Work even until armholes measure 5" from first underarm BO; end ready to work a RS row.

Shape Neck: Work across 10 (12, 12, 14, 16, 18) sts, BO 7 (5, 9, 7, 5, 5) sts, work remaining sts—10 (12, 12, 14, 16, 18) sts in each shoulder.

Attach second ball of yarn. Working both shoulders simultaneously, work even until shoulders measure 7 (7 ½, 8, 8 ½, 9, 9 ½)" from first underarm BO.

BO.

FINISHING

Sew right shoulder. Using smaller needles, pick up and knit 3 sts for every 4 rows and 1 st for every st around neck opening. Work Garter st for 2 rows. BO. Sew left shoulder.

Pick up and knit sts around armholes, and work trim as for neck opening. Sew side seams.

Press garment lightly.

ARM WARMERS

For several centuries, fine needlework was an essential skill for a girl to attain in order for her to create an appealing dowry. It was thought that a woman should put as little burden for her upkeep as possible on her new husband, and so a good dowry would contain enough linens and dressing items, all sewn and decorated by hand, for the first several years of marriage. Needless to say, hundreds of hours went into the production of these items. Fingerless gloves were an important item in the needlework bag, as they would allow a girl to continue working when the fire became low and the home grew cold.

While you may never use these cabled and bobbled silk/wool arm warmers for needlework, you'll find them useful as a fanciful accessory and for utilitarian purposes—try them when you're working on a computer in a chilly office or taking photos outdoors in cold weather.

FINISHED MEASUREMENTS
6½" long
8" circumference at lower edge
9½" circumference at upper edge

YARN
White Lies Designs Interlude (50% silk / 50% merino
  wool; 90 yards / 42 grams): 3 skeins antique pink

NEEDLES
One pair straight needles size US 7 (4.5 mm)
Change needle size if necessary to obtain correct gauge.

NOTIONS
Cable needle
Yarn needle

GAUGE
20 sts and 28 rows = 4" (10 cm) in Stockinette stitch
  (St st)

STITCH PATTERNS

mb (make bobble)
(K1, p1, k1, p1, k1, p1, k1) in next st, pass 2nd, 3rd, 4th, 5th, 6th, and 7th st on right-hand needle over 1st st and off needle.

2/1 RC (2-over-1 right cross)
Slip 1 st to cn, hold to back, k2, k1 from cn.

2/1 LC (2-over-1 left cross)
Slip 2 sts to cn, hold to front, k1, k2 from cn.

2/1 RPC (2-over-1 right purl cross)
Slip 1 st to cn, hold to back, k2, p1 from cn.

2/1 LPC (2-over-1 left purl cross)
Slip 2 sts to cn, hold to front, p1, k2 from cn.

Hollow Oak Cable
(from *A Treasury of Knitting Patterns* by Barbara G. Walker)
(panel of 17 sts; 20-row repeat) (See Chart)

Rows 1, 3, 5, and 19 (WS): K6, p5, k6.

Row 2: P6, mb, k3, mb, p6.

Rows 4 and 20: P6, k2, mb, k2, p6.

Row 6: P5, 2/1 RC, p1, 2/1 LC, p5.

Rows 7 and 17: K5, p2, k1, p1, k1, p2, k5.

Row 8: P4, 2/1 RPC, k1, p1, k1, 2/1 LPC, p4.

Rows 9 and 15: K4, p3, k1, p1, k1, p3, k4.

Row 10: P3, 2/1 RC, [p1, k1] 2 times, p1, 2/1 LC, p3.

Rows 11 and 13: K3, p2, [k1, p1] 3 times, k1, p2, k3.

Row 12: P3, k3, [p1, k1] 2 times, p1, k3, p3.

Row 14: P3, 2/1 LPC, [p1, k1] 2 times, p1, 2/1 RPC, p3.

Row 16: P4, 2/1 LPC, k1, p1, k1, 2/1 RPC, p4.

Row 18: P5, 2/1 LPC, p1, 2/1 RPC, p5.

Repeat Rows 1-20 for Hollow Oak Cable.

HOLLOW OAK CABLE

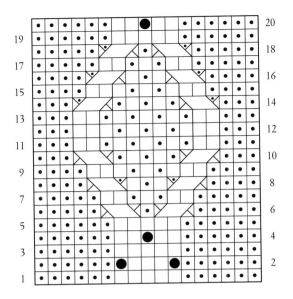

☐ KNIT ON RS, PURL ON WS

• PURL ON RS, KNIT ON WS

▱ 2/1 RC: SLIP NEXT ST TO CN, HOLD TO BACK, K2, K1 FROM CN

▱ 2/1 LC: SLIP NEXT 2 STS TO CN, HOLD TO FRONT, K1, K2 FROM CN

▱ 2/1 RPC: SLIP NEXT ST TO CN, HOLD TO BACK, K2, P1 FROM CN

▱ 2/1 LPC: SLIP NEXT 2 STS TO CN, HOLD TO FRONT, P1, K2 FROM CN

● MB: (K1, P1, K1, P1, K1, P1, K1) IN NEXT ST, PASS 2ND, 3RD, 4TH, 5TH, 6TH, AND 7TH ST ON RIGHT-HAND NEEDLE OVER 1ST ST AND OFF NEEDLE

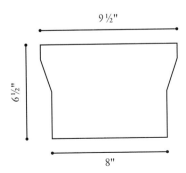

Mesh Pattern

(multiple of 3 sts + 3; 4-row repeat) (See Chart)

Rows 1 and 3 (WS): Purl.

Row 2: K2, *k2tog, yo, k1, repeat from *, end k1.

Row 4: K2, *yo, k1, k2tog, repeat from *, end k1.

Repeat Rows 1-4 for Mesh Pattern.

ARM WARMER (make 2)

CO 41 sts.

Row 1 (WS): Knit.

Row 2: K5, *mb, k4, repeat from *, end k1.

Row 3: Knit.

Row 4: Purl.

Next row, begin Mesh Pattern over next 12 sts, Hollow Oak Cable over following 17 sts, Mesh Pattern over last 12 sts.

Continuing in pattern as established, work even until arm warmer measures 3 ¼" from beginning.

Increase 1 st at each end of needle every 4 rows 4 times, working additional sts in St st—49 sts.

Work even until arm warmer measures approximately 6" from beginning; end having worked Row 2 of Hollow Oak Cable.

Next WS row, knit.

Next RS row, k4, *mb, k4, repeat from *.

Next WS row, knit.

BO in purl.

FINISHING

Sew back seam of arm warmer. Do not block.

MESH PATTERN

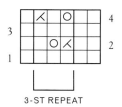

3-ST REPEAT

☐   KNIT ON RS, PURL ON WS

Ⓞ   YO

⎊   K2TOG

Special Techniques

CABLE CO (to cast on initial sts)

Make a loop (using a slip knot) with the working yarn and place it on the left-hand needle (first st CO). Knit into slip knot, draw up a loop but do not drop st from left-hand needle; place new loop on left-hand needle. *Insert the tip of the right-hand needle into the space between the last 2 sts on the left-hand needle and draw up a loop; place the loop on the left-hand needle. Repeat from * for remaining sts to be CO.

CABLE CO (to cast on additional sts at the end of a row)

Hold needle with sts in left hand, and empty needle in right hand. *Insert the tip of the right-hand needle into the space between the last 2 sts on the left-hand needle and draw up a loop; place the loop on the left-hand needle. Repeat from * for remaining sts to be CO.

CASING FOR ELASTIC

Using yarn needle and yarn, embroider a row of V's on inside of garment at instructed location. Make each V slightly taller than width of elastic, as illustrated. Embroider lightly on wrong side of fabric to ensure embroidery is invisible on right side.

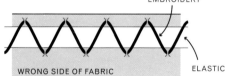

CROCHET CHAIN

Make a slip knot and place on hook, *yarn over and draw through loop on hook; repeat from * for desired length.

GARTER STITCH

Knit every row when working flat; knit 1 round, purl 1 round when working circularly.

I-CORD

Using double-pointed needles, cast on 3 sts. *Transfer needle with sts to left hand and bring yarn behind work to right-hand side; using second double-pointed needle, knit sts from right to left, pulling yarn from left to right for the first st; do not turn. Slide the sts to opposite end of needle; repeat from * until cord is length desired.

PICK UP AND KNIT

With RS of fabric facing, *insert right-hand needle from front to back into fabric at fabric edge, wrap yarn around needle as if to knit, and pull yarn forward through fabric to create a new stitch on the right-hand needle; repeat from * as instructed.

PROVISIONAL CO (crochet chain method)

Using a crochet hook and smooth yarn (crochet cotton or ravel cord used for machine knitting), work a crochet chain with a few more chains than the number of sts needed; fasten off. If desired, tie a knot on the fastened-off end to mark the end from which you will unravel later. Turn the chain over. Using project yarn and starting a few chains in from the beginning of the chain, pick up and knit one st in each bump at the back of the chain, leaving any extra chains at the end unworked. Continue as directed.

When ready to work the live sts, unravel the chain by loosening the fastened-off end and "unzipping" the chain, placing the live sts on a spare needle.

PROVISIONAL CO (waste yarn method)

Using waste yarn, CO the required number of sts. Work in Stockinette st for 3 or 4 rows, then work 1 row with a thin, smooth yarn (crochet cotton or ravel cord used for machine knitting) as a separator row. Change to project yarn and continue as directed.

When ready to work the live sts, pull out the separator row, placing the live sts on a spare needle.

READING CHARTS

When working flat, charts are read from right to left for RS rows and from left to right for WS rows. Numbers on the right indicate RS rows; numbers on the left indicate WS rows. When working circularly, all rounds are read from right to left.

REVERSE STOCKINETTE STITCH (rev St st)

Purl on RS rows, knit on WS rows when working flat; purl every round when working circularly.

RIBBING

Although rib stitch patterns use different numbers of sts, all are worked in the same way, whether working flat or circularly. The instructions will specify how many sts to knit or purl; the example below uses k1, p1.

Row 1: *K1, p1; repeat from * across (end k1 if an odd number of sts).

Row 2: Knit the knit sts and purl the purl sts as they face you.

Repeat Row 2 for rib st.

SHORT ROW SHAPING

Work the number of sts specified in the instructions, then wrap and turn (wrp-t) as follows: Bring yarn to front of work, slip the next st to the right-hand needle, bring yarn to back of work, return slipped st on right-hand needle to left-hand needle; turn, ready to work the next row, leaving remaining sts unworked.

When short rows are completed, or when working progressively longer short rows, work each wrap together with the st it wraps as follows: If st is to be knit, insert the right-hand needle into the wrap from below, then into the

wrapped st, then knit them together. If st to be purled, lift wrap onto the left-hand needle, then purl together with the wrapped st.

STOCKINETTE STITCH (St st)

Knit on RS rows, purl on WS rows when working flat; knit every round when working circularly.

STRAP ASSEMBLY

Attach ring to garment as instructed. Place slide on strap by weaving strap through slide as illustrated. Thread strap through ring as illustrated. Secure end of strap to center bar of slide by sewing with sewing needle and thread or yarn needle and yarn, as instructed.

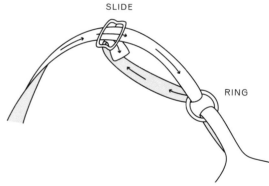

SLIDE

RING

SUSPENDER ASSEMBLY

Place slide on suspender strap by weaving strap through slide as illustrated. Thread strap through garter grip as illustrated. Secure end of strap to center bar of slide by sewing with sewing needle and thread or yarn needle and yarn, as instructed.

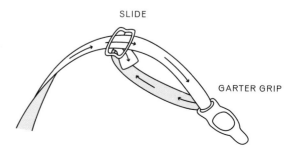

SLIDE

GARTER GRIP

Abbreviations

BO = Bind off.

CC = Contrast color.

ch = Chain.

cn = Cable needle.

CO = Cast on.

dc (double crochet) = Yarn over hook (2 loops on hook), insert hook into next stitch, yarn over hook and pull up a loop (3 loops on hook), [yarn over and draw through 2 loops] twice.

dpn(s) = Double-pointed needle(s).

hdc (half double crochet) = Yarn over hook (2 loops on hook), insert hook into next stitch, yarn over hook and draw up a loop (3 loops on hook), yarn over and draw through all 3 loops on hook.

k = Knit.

k2tog = Knit 2 sts together.

k3tog = Knit 3 sts together.

LH = Left hand.

M1 (make 1) = With the tip of the left-hand needle inserted from front to back, lift the strand between the two needles onto the left-hand needle; knit the strand through the back loop to increase one stitch.

MC = Main color.

p = Purl.

p2tog = Purl 2 sts together.

p3tog = Purl 3 sts together.

pm = Place marker.

Rev St st = Reverse Stockinette stitch.

RH = Right hand.

rnd(s) = Round(s).

RS = Right side.

RT (right twist) = Bring right-hand needle in front of first st on left-hand needle and knit second st, leaving both sts on left-hand needle; knit first st; drop both sts off left-hand needle.

sc (single crochet) = Insert hook into next st and draw up a loop (2 loops on hook), yarn over and draw through both loops on hook.

sl (slip) = Slip stitch(es) as if to purl, unless otherwise specified.

sl st (crochet slip stitch) = Insert hook in st, yarn over hook, and draw through loop on hook.

sm = Slip marker.

ssk (slip, slip, knit) = Slip the next 2 sts to the right-hand needle one at a time as if to knit; return them back to left-hand needle one at a time in their new orientation; knit them together through the back loops.

ssp (slip, slip, purl) = Slip the next 2 sts to right-hand needle one at a time as if to knit; return them to the left-hand needle one at a time in their new orientation; purl them together through the back loops.

St st = Stockinette stitch (see Special Techniques—Stockinette Stitch).

st(s) = Stitch(es).

trc = Yarn over hook twice (3 loops on hook), insert hook into next stitch, yarn over hook and pull up a loop (4 loops on hook), [yarn over and draw through 2 loops] 3 times.

wrp-t = Wrap and turn (see Special Techniques—Short Row Shaping).

WS = Wrong side.

yo = Yarn over.

Resources

YARNS

Berroco, Inc.
P.O. Box 367
14 Elmdale Road
Uxbridge, MA 01569
508-278-2527
www.berroco.com

Dancing Fibers
3305 66th Street #4
Lubbock, TX 79413
806-866-2673
www.dancingfibers.com

Cascade Yarns
1224 Andover Park E
Tukwila, WA 98188
800-548-1048
www.cascadeyarns.com

Classic Elite Yarns, Inc.
122 Western Avenue
Lowell, MA 01851
978-453-2837
www.classiceliteyarns.com

JCA Crafts, Inc.
35 Scales Lane
Townsend, MA 01469
978-597-8794
www.jcacrafts.com

Knit One, Crochet Too
91 Tandberg Trail, Unit 6
Windham, ME 04062
800-357-7646
www.knitonecrochettoo.com

Louet Sales
808 Commerce Park Drive
Ogdensburg, NY 13669
613-925-4502
www.louet.com

White Lies Designs
P.O. Box 214883
Sacramento, CA 95821
916-247-5580
www.whiteliesdesigns.com

NOTIONS

Elastics, ribbons, rosettes, tulle,
embroidery floss:

Hancock Fabrics
One Fashion Way
Baldwyn, MS 38824
877-322-7427
www.hancockfabrics.com

Jo-Ann
2361 Rosecrans Avenue, Suite 360
El Segundo, CA 90245
800-525-4951
www.joann.com

Fusible tricot interfacing, underwires,
hook-and-eye tape, channeling, strap
and garter findings:

White Lies Designs
P.O. Box 214883
Sacramento, CA 95821
916-247-5580
www.whiteliesdesigns.com

Acknowledgments

Special thanks to my husband, Mike, and son, Stuart, for their patience with me, and for their willingness to shuffle responsibilities during the creation of *Knitting Lingerie Style.*

Thanks to JC Briar for her razor-sharp tech-editing skills; to text editor Betty Christiansen for prompting me in just the right ways; to photographer Thayer Allyson Gowdy and stylist Karen Schaupeter and their amazing team for creating the extraordinary images; to graphic designer Anna Christian for pulling everything together so exquisitely; and to editor Melanie Falick for her vision, unfailingly good taste, and determination to keep me from sneaking any sequined pasties into this book.

My thanks also go out to the yarn companies who were so helpful in getting yarn to me promptly; to knitters Donna Warnell and Song Palmese for being so conscientious; and to Hélène Rush for her sage advice about book publishing. Also, my thanks to the powers in the boardroom at STC for taking a chance and rolling with a slightly different idea for a knitting book.

Last but not least, thanks to all the great knitters whom I've met in person and on the internet who have continually prompted me with "Hey Joan, you really should write a book."

I feel very grateful.

Index